# Poetic Lives: Dickinson

# Poetic Lives: Dickinson

Rebecca Swift

Poetic Lives
Published by Hesperus Press Limited
19 Bulstrode Street, London W1U 2JN
www.hesperuspress.com

First published by Hesperus Press Limited, 2011



Designed and typeset by Fraser Muggeridge studio
Printed in the UK by CPI William Clowes, Beccles, NR34 7TL

ISBN: 978-1-84391-306-1

# Contents

# *First – Poets – Then the Sun –* Overview

When Emily Dickinson died her sister Lavinia, who had shared a house with her, found forty home-made volumes of poems among her very few possessions. In addition to these small booklets (also known as fascicles) – largely written in pen, some in pencil, many of them, in Lavinia's words, 'tied together with twine' – were many more poems written on a variety of different sheets and scraps of paper, left outside the booklets. Her patterns of recording and collecting her own work varied in different years but, roughly, she began the practice of collation when she was twenty-seven years old in 1858 and continued intensively until 1863, and then more intermittently until her death, aged fifty-five, in 1886.

This secret cache of 1,789 poems discovered to date, left behind after the poet's death, constituted a hoard of literary treasure that in time would ensure that its author became one of the most celebrated writers in the world. This is true to the extent that the contemporary American poet and critic Adrienne Rich claimed she described psychological states better than anybody 'except Shakespeare.'

During her lifetime, however, Emily had no public profile other than the reputation she had gained within a small circle. She had achieved this by sending poems in letters, in various drafts, to different friends, extended family and a few influential others. While she lived, she had, for some of those who knew her, obtained something of a mythical status, not only on the strength of the power of the body of work she circulated in this informal manner, but also because of the brilliance and eccentricity of her personality.

People are intrigued by the fact that, despite a vivacious childhood and young adulthood, Emily by her mid-thirties had become a virtual recluse. She stayed within the confines of the house and grounds known as the Homestead that she shared chiefly with Lavinia, and various cats and servants, and controlled meetings with others on her own sometimes bizarre terms. Different commentators have offered a range of explanations for Emily's reclusive tendencies, yet it is best to make it clear at the outset that Emily Dickinson will remain a mystery. This is part of her enduring fascination. Emily herself left only the poems and letters, and was deliberately elliptical and by nature paradoxical. Unlike other writers whose craft leaps out beyond the bounds of the formal poetical style of their age – great experimentalists and originals such as Walt Whitman, Gerard Manley Hopkins, Ezra Pound or E.E. Cummings – Emily left no articulated aesthetic of her work: why she wrote as she did, or what she was trying to achieve.

One of her biographers, John Cody, refers to her life as being ruptured by a 'psychological cataclysm', and comments that trying to interpret precisely what happened to her, would be like trying to work out what had happened to an aircraft that had exploded mid-flight. This is a strong way of expressing the period of breakdown Emily is thought to have suffered at some time between 1857 and 1862, most potently articulated during an outburst of creative activity during the years 1861–3. The technological imagery Cody employs may seem odd, except that Emily herself viewed part of her mind as a machine that had the potential to go wrong. In a letter of early 1856 to her friend Mrs J.G. (Elizabeth Luna Chapin) Holland she writes, 'I often wish I was a grass, or a toddling daisy, whom all these problems of the dust might not terrify – and should my own machinery get slightly out of gear, *please*, kind ladies and gentlemen, some one stop the wheel, –'

One of the many reasons that Emily Dickinson strikes a chord with such a large readership is that there is something about her story that appeals to our own sense of the possibility of being 'discovered' after we have died: the hope that this life does not hold all that there is to have. This notion can be of solace. While she lived no more than ten (possibly eleven) of Emily's poems were published – and these, with one exception, without her permission. Emily Dickinson seems both to have held a firm belief in the worth and enduring merit of her own work, and at the same time to have had a highly fragile sense of self-worth.

Despite many hints at symbolic 'marriages', the nature of which we shall explore, we can be certain that Emily's most committed relationship was with poetry and words: as she writes in an undated poem, her 'loved Philology'. The intensity of her bond with language is made explicit by her appropriation of the Bible.

*A word made Flesh is seldom*
*And tremblingly partook*
*Nor then perhaps reported*
*But have I not mistook*
*Each one of us has tasted*
*With ecstasies of stealth*
*The very food debated*
*To our specific strength –*

*A word that breathes distinctly*
*Has not the power to die*
*Cohesive as the Spirit*
*It may expire if He –*

*"Made Flesh and dwelt among us"*
*Could condescension be*
*Like this consent of Language*
*This loved Philology*

In another poem, one of her strongest, from 1863, Emily expresses her overweening passion for, and belief in, poetry; claiming 'First – Poets – Then the Sun –':

> *I reckon – When I count at all –*
> *First – Poets – Then the Sun –*
> *Then Summer –Then the Heaven of God –*
> *And then – the List is done –*
>
> *But, looking back – the First so seems*
> *To Comprehend the Whole –*
> *The Others look a needless Show –*
> *So I write – Poets – All –*

We shall explore Emily's story in this brief life, but the reader should remember that this poet's life was even more peculiarly internal than that of most poets, and her relationship with words libidinal and unique. External events, such as the Civil War of 1861–5, were arguably marginal to her, as we shall see. At the same time, the tension and drama of some of her verse during those years echo the larger political picture, even if these are not the expressed themes. Whatever her subject, it was the richness and peculiarity of her mental life and the singularity of her relationship with words that made this poet what she was. Emily Dickinson, for better or worse, conducted her main relationship to the world through letters and poetic communications sent in letters to a wide variety of intimates – both men and women.

Emily explored the mind at all levels, conscious and unconscious, recording in poems various dreams and fantasies, making it difficult sometimes to separate what might have been a 'real' external event from a powerful internal one symbolised in the work. Even in her letters her internal world could become so dominant that it sometimes bemused the recipient of the letter. Moreover, Emily asked her sister Vinnie to burn, after her death, all letters sent to her, and except for a few that escaped this conflagration or which may yet emerge, we are without letters sent back to Emily in response, so the remaining correspondence is largely one-sided. And as Emily did not date her poems, we cannot be sure of their dates.

Confronting these difficulties, scholars have reworked a chronology for the poetry using the order of notebooks Emily herself left, and by grouping the work around handwriting, theme and style. To complicate matters further, Emily sometimes wrote several drafts of the same work, and sent them to different people – at the same or different times. It was as if her hoard of writing was an ongoing project, a canvas that she worked and reworked over her lifetime, and of which there can never be a neat, finished picture. Emily's inner life and her work were intimately bound together, her relationship to things at once real and also highly coloured by her own projections and symbolic language.

Providing a precise and chronological but also meaningful account of such a life, relatively brief as it was, is therefore not straightforward. This is not only because of the difficulty of dating meetings, the one-sided correspondence, and a practised secrecy in respect of some of her own communications, but also because some apparently minor external events seem to take on extreme proportions in her inner world. A trip to church turns into a traumatic episode, as does a visit from a man on whom she may have projected the biggest emotional experience of her life, whereas other events (such as her withdrawal from a once good friend) can seem hardly to trouble her. The unconscious mind was said by Freud to have no time and no contradictions; this can sometimes seem true of the conscious life of Emily Dickinson, and is certainly true of her poetic work. Even when expressing the darkest thoughts, she can write an apparently innocent nature poem full of joy; even when racked with extremes, she can find a pocket of peace.

Perhaps it is not surprising that not more biographers have tackled the subject of Emily Dickinson. Her poems are difficult, and material about her life is elusive. But we can attempt to approach her through her work, and perhaps foreshadow what we can discover of her story with a glimpse of her childhood, seen through a poem written in 1862, when she was thirty-one years old.

In 'I was the slightest in the House –', she looks back at her childhood through a certain lens, positioning herself as a passive child who takes up little space, but does listen to the conversation of others, which she absorbs quietly. She describes the conversation as 'the mint' – i.e. money – and says that there was a constant flow of it, for her to 'catch'. She sits with her little basket listening, and the suggestion is that the girl's ordinary domestic item becomes a container for the verbal nuggets that pour from the others. For a woman who was economically dependent all her life and who never worked for money, the frequent use of financial imagery in her work is striking. The young Emily's position is an intriguing one, and one that represents something elemental about her and also paradoxical: for while she is diminutive, silent and barely noticed, she is also in a position of great power as the recipient of 'the mint' that falls almost effortlessly into her domain. Mental and poetic wealth as weighed against other kinds of wealth, marital or financial, are themes she returns to again and again. In later life she removed herself from direct contact with most people, even friends, but would sometimes listen to their conversations from behind a half-open door. Still addicted to the verbal (and on occasion musical) 'mint', she became addicted also to the position of diminutive outsider, to the quiet, removed life. Some would say she lived in the hermetical in the tradition of the religious devotee. In the poem, while others talked, and whilst she is prepared to benefit from this talk, she herself 'could not bear to live – aloud', as the noise made her feel ashamed. Yet Emily's position was again one of paradox, displaying superiority, and disdain, as well as dependency. Here, the poem under discussion ends with the comment that despite the sense of quiet superiority the 'I' in the poem has, she often reflects that she could die without anybody noticing, or caring. Fear of disappearing, of being forgotten, of having no legacy are also potent themes throughout her life, juxtaposed with a fundamental if faltering security that she has somehow garnered enough of 'the mint' to be immortalised forever through her art. Emily wrote a few poems about her childhood, all retrospective. The one we are discussing is worth citing in full and will lead us to an account of what we know or can deduce about the family background and influences into which this exceptional child was born.

*I was the slightest in the House –*
*I took the smallest Room –*
*At night, my little Lamp, and Book –*
*And one Geranium –*

*So stationed I could catch the mint*
*That never ceased to fall –*
*And just my Basket –*
*Let me think – I'm sure*
*That this was all –*

*I never spoke – unless addressed –*
*And then, 'twas brief and low –*
*I could not bear to live – aloud –*
*The Racket shamed me so –*

*And if it had not been so far –*
*And any one I knew*
*Were going – I had often thought*
*How noteless – I could die –*

## *I was the slightest in the House* – Background and early years

Emily Dickinson was born into one of the most influential families in Amherst, a small, prosperous, relatively new country town in the state of Massachusetts, New England, America, at 5 a.m. on 10th December 1830. Biographer Richard B. Sewall records that her grandfather, Samuel Fowler Dickinson, was considered by one of his daughters, probably Elizabeth, 'gentle and sensitive, and with more than ordinary mental gifts'. Thirty-one years earlier, he had helped to build the town Emily lived and died in. Samuel Fowler was also an ardent, pioneering man, who fathered nine children with his wife Lucretia Gunn. He came from English stock, and two centuries before his grand-daughter arrived his forebears had left Lincolnshire, along with many others, in search of a new life in which they could continue to practise Protestantism without endangering their lives: in England at that time persecution of Protestants was rife under the divided reign of Charles I. By the time Emily was born, because the Dickinsons had been active for generations in the fertile area in which Amherst was founded, the Dickinson name was well established, as was the family reputation for 'Dickinson grit'.

Emily's grandfather, by all accounts no ordinary man, although 'gentle', was nonetheless a proponent of a form of severe Calvinist orthodoxy, a faith which contained elements of violent extremity. The legacy of this extreme religious landscape can be seen at work in Emily's poetic imagination. Even though Dickinson herself – remarkably given the pressure she was under to conform – never committed to belief in a strictly Protestant God, she nonetheless explores repeatedly the subject and meaning of God; of immortality, faith and the afterlife. Theological mint was certainly among the riches that fell her way. Her basket caught the religious language of her forebears and her poetic style absorbed its preoccupations and extremes, although from it she was to make a language unique to herself, in a way that modern readers particularly admire.

Two acts of Samuel Fowler Dickinson were to have a direct impact on the poet: the first is that in 1813 he built the Homestead, which is thought to be the first brick house in Amherst.

The Homestead, or Dickinson family mansion, was the house that was to become so important to the poet: the house in which she was born and in which she would die. It was her haven, and in some respects her 'prison', as she posits in a poem of 1862, 'A Prison gets to be a friend –'. The Homestead became a place of particular importance to Emily Dickinson, but it should be remembered that there was a long period of fifteen years during which she did not live there. Difficulties created by Samuel Fowler's overextended financial support of Amherst College and then his death in 1838 caused Emily's father to move the family. Between the ages of nine and twenty-four (1840–55) the poet lived in a house on West Street, which was later renamed North Pleasant. This house is no longer standing, having been covered by a petrol station in 1920, and another one after, which is there to this day.

The Homestead, however, is still there today and is now open to the public. Movingly preserved, it is a shrine to the poet, and houses the white dress that she began to wear almost exclusively, as well as the engravings of George Eliot and Elizabeth Barrett Browning and the small desk she often wrote at. There also, poised on a ledge by the window in her bedroom, is her lidded, handled basket made of woven strips of unidentified wood, in which she used to lower gingerbread to her nephew and niece, and perhaps the same one that she imagined catching 'mint'. Along a short path several hundred yards in length stands the Evergreens, a second property built on Dickinson ground by Emily's father. The poet's brother Austin and his wife Susan Huntington Gilbert moved in to this impressive mansion in 1856. Their relationship plays a major part in Emily's story. The Evergreens also still stands today: a grand house with a haunted feeling. The nursery, the room Emily's nephew Gilbert tragically died in aged seven, is still as he left it with a suit of clothes on the bed and with his toys out. When I visited in 2005, the wallpaper hung heavy with damp, the atmosphere was thick. The tour-guide reported that Susan Gilbert Dickinson's daughter, Martha, had asked her heir Alfred Leete Hampson that the house be 'razed' to the ground rather than left intact if it be sold outside the family.

The second significant act of Emily's grandfather; aside from building the Homestead; was co-founding Amherst College and the associated school, Amherst Academy, which Emily attended on and off for seven years. Built in part in order to help protect Calvinism against the growing, softer Unitarianism, the school was to be a major influence on Emily.

Emily Dickinson's own father, Edward, was one of nine much-loved children of Samuel and his wife Lucretia Gunn. Samuel Fowler achieved a good deal, and yet there was also a reckless strain to his personality that seems to have bordered on the manic: a trait we see echoed in Emily's more private but nonetheless volatile and intellectually pioneering personality. Samuel Fowler forged forward, creating towns, institutions for education and the family mansion; his granddaughter created an empire of words. Both lives paid heavy costs for their courage. In Samuel Fowler's case he led his family into debt and a financial crisis, the after-effects of which were to impact directly on Edward.

Forbidding in temperament and conservative, Edward seems to have reacted to Samuel Fowler's brilliant but destabilising excesses by becoming anxious and protective, both a clinging and, paradoxically, a remote father. Whilst there are several references to his having a stern personality, Emily also refers in her letters to her father's not being able to do without her at home, using this as a reason not to travel to see people. When Emily was young, Edward also kept her out of school on grounds of ill-health for prolonged periods of time. A combination of his fear for her well-being, a need for her presence and a desire to build a Dickinson stronghold where the precious family line could be kept safe and true to itself seem to have contributed to Emily's view as she grew older that home was the only place to be. An almost incestuous sense of superiority also seems to have existed among the Dickinsons and the Dickinson arrogance is well noted; when writing to her future sister-in-law Susan Gilbert, on 9th October 1851, Emily comments that her family has the 'fancy that we are the only poets, and everyone else is *prose*'.

Determined to build a stable reputation and home, Edward worked hard and became an attorney and highly respected and responsible figure in Amherst. Like his father, he was involved in many areas of civic life, was briefly elected to stand as parliamentary representative at national level for an independent party, and was actively involved in bringing the railway to Amherst. Emily observes a train moving off at a celebration of the new line's opening in a letter to Austin of 13th June 1853, and in a vivid, later poem she brings the locomotive alive:

*I like to see it lap the Miles –*
*And lick the Valleys up –*
*And stop to feed itself at Tanks –*
*And then – prodigious step*

Edward's attitude to women represented a doublebind typical of many men of the period. Though he clearly believed that they should be educated, at the same time he feared that books 'joggle the Mind'. A woman's proper place was in the home, enabling men to exercise their duties and build their place in the world. It is doubtful that he ever realised what he had produced in Emily, who took care to continue with the domestic routines, baking bread (as had a heroine of hers, Emily Brontë) and along with her sister helping the servants. It was not unusual for middle-class families to support the work of a small domestic staff, and the Dickinson wife and daughters did this throughout their lives, when health allowed. We should remember that a share in the work of the household, fire-building, cooking (which her niece Martha later said she attended to with the same focus she applied to her writing), gardening and even entertaining her father's colleagues and friends, made up the poet's daily rounds. As she became more sequestered, these duties (and pleasures) remained in place, alongside the writing that appears to have offered her a virtually constant source of mental exercise and inspiration. She shared her writing with some, most importantly her sister-in-law Susan, for example, but the seriousness of this activity was probably kept quiet from her father. In front of him his children were respectful, yet behind his back they would often subside into giggles. Emily was, as family records testify, a wonderful mimic. Dutiful yet playful and rebellious, Emily found a way to be both a loving daughter and her own remarkable self within her patriarchal home.

Edward's attitude to women was reflected in his choice of wife, whom Emily described to her close correspondent Thomas Wentworth Higginson (acerbically) as not caring 'for thought'. Significantly, we know less about Emily Norcross than about her husband. She was a mild, nervous woman from Monson, Massachuesetts, who had lost four siblings in childhood, retaining only one, later Aunt Lavinia, into adulthood. She was won over by the persistency of the courtship letters Edward sent, and upset about having to abandon the care of her mother when she left to get married. There is some evidence that Emily was more like her mother than she and some commentators have thought: for example, the elder Emily wrote a brief love note to a teacher to whom her daughter later became attached, and also wrote a letter with a metaphor in it that echoes an element of Emily's style. Nonetheless, evidence suggests that mother and her literary daughter never formed a highly identified bond. As a mother, Emily Norcross was prone to apply herself to almost obsessive domestic activity, and then to suffer bouts of depression, with a severe, long-term episode beginning in 1855, the year that Edward moved the family back to the Homestead from West Street. It may have been that as with many housewives, her intelligence and passions were subsumed by childcare, duty and domesticity, such suppression being a source of depression in women historically. It may also have been that she never recovered from early sibling losses of her own, and from being separated from her beloved sister Lavinia (Emily's adored aunt), and her mother, about whose death she felt guilty.

When Emily Dickinson was born that December in 1830, she already had an older brother who was only twenty months her senior. William Austin, known as Austin, was extremely precious to Emily. He, and his marriage, would play a critical part in her life. Two years and three months after Emily's birth, the family was completed by the arrival of a third child, Lavinia Dickinson; the loving, also eccentric but more practical sister who was to become a critical companion to Emily, and with whom she shared a house all her life (along with various cats and for a long period a dog called Carlo, a Newfoundland bought as a companion for Emily in 1849).

There is one significant story from the poet's toddler-hood that is worth exploring, and which might perhaps shed some light on Emily's relation to her mother. It also illuminates Emily's acute anxiety about separation. This afflicted her all her life, so much so that there is a strong argument that fear of loss was a contributing factor to her increasing desire to control relationships on her own terms, and to her marked avoidance of seeing people face-to-face as she grew older.

When Lavinia – known often as Vinnie – was born, her mother was struggling. Whatever the reasoning, Emily was sent away to help ease the burden of having to look after both girls. It was far more common then for babies to be sent to stay with relatives, sometimes for extended periods of time, than it is now, but nonetheless subsequent research, such as that undertaken by attachment theorist John Bowlby in the 1950s and beyond, about the effects of early separation and other causes of anxiety in the very young, does indicate that an extended period of time away from your mother particularly before the age of five can be a contributing factor in subsequent separation anxiety.

When the two-and-a-half-year-old Emily and her aunt left Amherst in a carriage to go to Monson, there was a tremendous storm through which they continued to ride in the carriage. Emily was frightened. Aunt Lavinia recorded that at first Emily 'felt inclined to be frightened some – she said "Do take me to my mother" But I covered her face all under my cloak to protect her & took care that she did not get wet much –' Emily, apparently (in her first recorded words), called the lightning 'the fire'. In a poem of 1862, one of Emily's most prolific years, she writes:

*It struck me – every Day –*
*The Lightning was as new*
*As if the Cloud that instant slit*
*And let the Fire through –*

Might the lightning in this poem have been in part made up of an early memory? The poem continues, describing how the lightning has been persecuting her in a dream.

*It burned Me – in the Night –*
*It Blistered to My Dream –*
*It sickened fresh opon my sight –*
*With every Morn that came –*

Like Prometheus, whose fate it was to be punished for stealing fire from the gods by being bound to a rock and having his renewed liver plucked out every day by vultures, the subject of the poem suffers from endlessly renewable pain. The poem concludes uncannily:

*I thought that Storm – was brief –*
*The Maddest – quickest by –*
*But Nature lost the Date of This –*
*And left it in the Sky –*

Psychoanalyst Melanie Klein convincingly posited that human beings begin to symbolise while babies. Where loved ones are absent, imaginative representation steps in. This process can be benign if the child feels sufficiently secure, as in the case of Proust's madeleines, or terrifying if the gap represents a dread and subsequent distortion of 'mother' to something terrifying, as with Emily's lightning.

After her arrival at her aunt and uncle's house when a toddler, Emily apparently settled down and became very placid and pleasant. Lavinia wrote to Emily's mother that the child was 'perfectly contented'; that she 'speaks of her father & mother occasionaly & *little Austin* but does not express a wish to see you –'. Emily might have settled down, or she might, as some argue, have been behaving like a good little girl, while masking a high level of anxiety at the pain of being excluded from her mother's world at such a critical time. If we are to take her reactions to the absence of those she loved in later life as evidence of an emotional template (and there are striking repetitions in her reactions, as we will see), it is almost impossible not to conclude that her nature and the way it interacted with external reality caused her to be unusually sensitive to loss and absence, which was so often presumed by her to be active neglect.

When Emily was thirty-nine, years after she wrote the lightning poem, Higginson, a writer, editor and campaigner with whom she had developed a significant correspondence on the subject of her own writing, recorded various questions and statements that the fascinating poet had made upon the occasion of his visit to Amherst. Among these were, 'Could you tell me what home is' and 'I never had a mother. I suppose a mother is one to whom you hurry when you are troubled.' It is remarkable that Emily Dickinson, who never left her adhesively close family, who shared one half of a large house with her sister, the other half being occupied by her parents, was the same person that asks a relative stranger what a home is.

There is a large element of attitudinising in her letters to Higginson, almost as if she were posing as a person of mythical quality in order to attract attention. Yet the theme of being parentless is repeated in a more ordinary relationship.

Writing to Elizabeth Holland, one of her most stable and enduring friends and the wife of the influential founder of *Scribner's Monthly* Josiah Gilbert Holland, Emily makes a comment worthy of note. Albeit both parents by now old, Emily's comment echoes others made earlier. She says, 'I was thinking of thanking you for the kindness to Vinnie. She has no Father and Mother but me and I have no Parents but her.'

It is also to Elizabeth Holland that Emily makes the much-cited comment about her mother following her death in a letter of mid-December 1882. This shows that as her mother grew weaker with age, Emily was able to feel closer to her:

> *Mother has now been gone five Weeks... We were never intimate Mother and Children while she was our Mother – but Mines in the same Ground meet by tunneling and when she became our Child, the Affection came – When we were Children and she journeyed, she always brought us something. Now, would she bring us but herself, what an only Gift – Memory is a strange Bell ...*

One last observation before we move on to her schooling is that Emily suffered another disturbance when she was three years old.

At that time, Edward and his family shared the Homestead with his parents. In 1833, the erratic Samuel Fowler sold up his half of the Homestead that he had built, to take up a job training an orthodox clergy at a new seminary in Cincinnati, Ohio. This was in order to help reduce his debts. He left Amherst along with his wife and two of Emily's aunts, selling his part of the house to General David Mack. At this point Emily's family moved from the west half of the house to the east, where Edward's parents had been: an unexpected loss and a psychic shift within the same four walls.

In 1838, when Emily was seven, Samuel Fowler died in Hudson, Ohio. According to his daughter Catherine, her father's 'spirits' were 'completely broken' from 'anxiety & care & disappointment'. Edward was compelled to sell his own half of the Dickinson mansion. The family would move back, but not for fifteen years.

The move out of the Homestead to West Street, made when Emily was nine, appears to have been a positive one for the women in the family. The house was spacious, and did not have to be shared with ancient family members or generals. It is true that from the second window Amherst's burial ground, described as 'forbidding' and 'repulsive' by a local minister, was a source of both playful and morbid preoccupation for Emily, but the house also afforded them a beautiful garden, orchard, grapevines and pine trees – and became a place that drew in visitors and guests. Some of these guests became early friends and sources of involvement for Emily.

The Dickinson household was busy with comings and goings of Amherst society, and Edward, very much a man of the world, would have had many visitors. When Emily was growing up it seems that she was anything but a recluse. She was exposed to the conversation and preoccupations of some of the best male minds in the neighbourhood, and as a woman of the household she would have been expected to help entertain, a duty she continued to perform when she could throughout her life. Much of 'the mint' caught in her basket fell from the lips of visiting guests. She was also inspired by the sermons of an impressive new preacher, Reverend Aaron Merrick Colton, who came to Amherst in 1840 and remained a favourite of Edward Dickinson for many years.

Stimulation was also provided by house guests such as Joseph Bardwell Lyman, a likeable young man who flirted with the girls and had a love affair with Vinnie; Benjamin Franklin Newton, a highly intelligent young man who came to stay for two years as a protégé of Edward; and also Jane Humphrey, who stayed while she was attending Amherst Academy. While she stayed, Jane shared a bed with Emily, and Emily never forgot their closeness. This was expressed years later in a high-octane letter to Jane, written at a time when Emily feared that she was losing her future sister-in-law Sue's affection, and when other valued friends were leaving Amherst. There is not time here fully to explore all of her relationships, other than the most important; but suffice to say, Emily did not lack company or stimulation.

## *'you know I am always in love with my teachers'* Emily at school

While still at the Homestead, Emily attended a local primary school between the ages of four and eight, from 1835 to 1839, though which one exactly is unknown. Here, she would have learned basic arithmetic, spelling and grammar. It is worth noting that while we know that lectures about the importance of the correct usage of English grammar were being collected in publications for use in schools, and while Emily's own father seemed preoccupied with this theme, Emily and her brother as well as other contemporaries seem to have adopted what we consider eccentric grammatical usage today. Here is a quote from an 1838 lecture by R.G. Parker, collated in a series for the American Institute of Instruction, Boston, 1839:

> The rules of Grammar are all drawn from the usage of those whose writings have adorned the literature of their country, and shone as lights of their age. In order that a language may become fixed, or acquire any degree of permanency, it is absolutely necessary that some forms of expression should be established and deviations from them rejected...

Yet Emily's own grammatical usage, in her poetry and letters, remained particularly idiosyncratic. This erratic usage is now considered a hallmark of her genius and originality and has been the subject of much scholarly debate.

Originality and individuality were of vital importance to Emily. Writing to a best friend who had left Amherst, some six years after leaving primary school, Emily warned against 'prim, starched up' young lady teachers, and urged, 'don't let your free spirit be chained by them.' The teachers Emily came to admire were at Amherst Academy, the establishment her own grandfather had helped bring into being, which Emily and Vinnie first attended as day students in 1840 when Emily was nine years old. While the associated Amherst College had developed as a serious religious institution set up in part to train missionaries, the Academy was run along liberal principles. The school was highly thought of, especially in the sciences and, particularly for the women, literature. It was because of a terrible fire that raged through Amherst in 1838 burning the local Female Seminary that Emily, or any girls, found themselves in attendance at Amherst. Around 100 were enrolled in the previously all-male establishment when Emily attended. Among the subjects on offer were botany, Latin, algebra, geology, history, ecclesiastical history, 'Mental Philosophy', arithmetic and geometry. Most importantly perhaps for our purposes, also on offer was, to use Emily's own phrase, 'Speaking and Composition'. The school day began and ended with prayer, and became the source of much pleasure as well as learning for the developing poet.

'I have very distinct and pleasant impressions of Emily Dickinson,' wrote Daniel T. Fiske, a teacher of Emily's in the years 1842–3. His recollections, provided almost fifty years later, give us an important portrait of the developing writer at that time. He went on:

> I remember her as a very bright, but rather delicate and frail looking girl; an excellent scholar, of exemplary deportment, faithful in all school duties; but somewhat shy and nervous. Her compositions were strikingly original; and in both thought and style seemed beyond her years,

> and always attracted much attention in the school and, I am afraid, excited not a little envy.

Emily herself seems to share her teacher's enthusiasm for her skill at composition. Writing to a close friend, Abiah Root, of whom we shall see more shortly, Emily writes in the letter recently quoted, in a slightly manic high-spirited strain on 7th May 1845, 'I have written one composition this term, and I need not assure you that it was exceedingly edifying to myself as well as everybody else. Don't you want to see it? I really wish you could have a chance.'

Amherst Academy was a source of stimulation and pleasure for the unusually gifted girl. In this scintillating letter, Emily also arrogantly but playfully declares:

> *I am growing handsome very fast indeed! I expect I shall be the belle of Amherst when I reach my 17th year. I don't doubt that I shall have perfect crowds of admirers at that age. Then how I shall delight to make them await my bidding, and with what delight shall I witness their suspense while I make my final decision.*

This shows us that at fourteen Emily was not preparing for a life of solitude. Indeed, social life was vital and at school Emily gathered around her a group of intimate friends. These included the other members of the gang of 'five' she refers to in her letters: Abiah Palmer Root, who came from the nearby hamlet of Springfield and was the daughter of a merchant and congregational deacon; Abby Maria Wood, who had lost her father and lived with an occasional correspondent of Emily's, Luke Sweetser, on the hill just north of the Dickinsons; Harriet Merril and Sarah S. Tracy.

Enthusiasm for her friends was topped only by the adoration Emily felt for many of her teachers. If Emily's teachers admired her mind, we know that she admired many of them in return;

the pupil-teacher relationship became a crucial one for the poet and continued to be so throughout her life. We have a particular record of admiration for a twenty-year-old teacher, Rebecca M. Woodbrige, about whom Emily wrote also to Abiah on 14th March 1847, aged sixteen. She describes in detail the teacher's beautiful physical appearance, and there is reference here also to "Our dear Miss Adams". Elizabeth C. Adams, the teacher under whose influence the 'five' had grown close, had left, it turned out temporarily, to get married at the end of 1846.

> *We all love her [Miss R. Woodbridge] very much... Forgive my glowing description, for you know I am always in love with my teachers. Yet, much as we love her, it seems lonely & strange without "Our dear Miss Adams."*

We know that Miss Adams held Emily in affection also, for she once sent her a 'newspaper as large as life' and a 'beautiful little bunch of pressed flowers'.

There were also some brilliant men at Amherst Academy, some of whom influenced Emily significantly. One of the most notable was Edward Hitchcock, eminent scientist and poet, author of several inspiring books (with less inspirational titles perhaps), *Catalogue of Plants Growing Without Cultivation in the Vicinity of Amherst College* (1829), *Elementary Geology* (1840), *Religious Lectures on Peculiar Phenomena in the Four Seasons* (1850) and *The Religion of Geology and its Connected Sciences* (1851). Sewall among others argues persuasively for Hitchcock's place in shaping the mind and language of the future poet. He points out that Emily turns words such as 'parallax' and 'perihelion' to 'vivid poetic use' in her work. These are two unlikely words that Emily uses in the poems 'I thought that nature was enough', and 'Delights Despair at setting'.

Sewall's point about Dickinson's debt to her scientific education and to her teacher is fully exemplified in her difficult poem 'The Lilac is an ancient Shrub', which is quite unlike any other 'flower poetry' of the period: here she seems to be using the colour of the shrub, and the mnemonic chime with the lilac in the sunset ('Opon the Hill Tonight') as a starting point for a metaphysical contemplation of the origins of the universe and the nature of eternity.

> *The Lilac is an ancient Shrub*
> *But ancienter than that*
> *The Firmamental Lilac*
> *Opon the Hill Tonight –*
> *The Sun subsiding on his Course –*
> *Bequeathes this final plant*
> *To Contemplation – not to Touch –*
> *The Flower of Occident.*

The 'Firmamental Lilac' (of the sunset) becomes a metaphorical flower, which provokes contemplation, although it cannot be touched. The poem continues with a dazzling display of botanic imagery, including the words 'Calyx', 'Capsule' and 'Seeds', and concludes with a warning that theologians, or theological rationalists perhaps (even those like Hitchcock himself who use the detail of science as further evidence of God as ingenious maker), be careful lest that which should be apprehended as mystery is pinned down too much, and the essence, only available as mysterious, direct experience, is lost. She reasons that:

> *The Scientist of Faith*
> *His research... just begun –*

will miss

> *The Flora unimpeachable*
> *To Time's Analysis –*

Real meaning will flower beyond the judgment or comprehension of our known framework and time frame, 'Above… Synthesis', on a higher plane than the new research of collated ideas about science and God can apprehend.

This complex poem serves, serendipitously, as an example of the kind of verbal detail Emily employs and the unusual vocabulary from which she draws: again, this precision is another hallmark of her genius and of the intensity of her relationship with her 'loved Philology'. Poems about the natural world abound in the poet's work, and she brings that world to us in her own distinctive manner. Some of the subjects – birds, snakes, spiders – may be conventional, but the treatment is not. Her distinctly unfeminine use of scientific language and her extreme accuracy of description are startling. Here was a poet who would not be chained to tradition and poetic niceties; nor to form. She gleaned the language she needed, the visions of the world she would bestow, from all who inspired her in the flesh, or from her reading.

The fascination with flowers was something that we know Emily possessed from an early age, and her collection of plants became a chief occupation. In January 1846, just fifteen, Emily wrote about the 'principal round of my occupation' as involving music lessons, two hours' practice a day, German lessons and 'a large stand of plants to cultivate'. In a sentimental painting made of the Dickinson family in 1840 by the artist Otis A. Bullard (one of only three images we have of Dickinson), he shows the artist with red hair, holding a flower above a book, which is open and revealing a flower. Emily's mother was a proficient and dedicated gardener, and Emily learned from her and went on to cultivate her own herbarium. She was so keen and skilled at this that her father bought her a conservatory in which she could grow her own local plants, and experiment with tropical plants not native to the region. Emily kept a bound book in which she recorded with the utmost care the names of almost four hundred varieties of flora, and which she pressed expertly, such as six species of

Narcissus (including *Narcissus poeticus*), *Verbena aubletia* and *Lupinus pilosus*. The Latin names are precisely employed. The extreme beauty of flowers, their constant renewal and death, the process of creation they made manifest, was a source of rich contemplation and pleasure for the writer. In 2006 a beautiful facsimile edition of Emily Dickinson's herbarium was published, and it contains three interesting essays about the impact of flower study on Emily's mind and work. 'The immortality of Flowers,' she wrote to Mrs (Sarah Eliza) Edward Tuckerman, when she had sent her half of a bouquet, 'must enrich our own.' Sewall goes further, and argues passionately, 'Take Emily's herbarium far enough and you have her.'

Another male teacher who made an impact on Emily was a young man, still a final-year student, who took over as acting principal in 1846. Leonard Humphrey was successful in his role, and helped to make the school more stable. Our knowledge about his relationship with Emily is mainly posthumous, for he died shockingly of brain congestion in 1850, and Emily wrote a letter of the same year that immortalises him, to which we will return later. However, of significance is that she makes reference to Leonard as her first 'Master'. Emily sought all of her life for figures who might teach her. As we look at her life with hindsight, and from a perspective that is almost aerial, allowing us to see patterning on a map of a life already lived and framed, we can see that the choice of the word 'Master' is significant terminology indeed.

To her chagrin, there were considerable periods when Emily did not attend school because of ill-health. Coughs plagued her, despite her father's efforts to protect his family from the danger of ailments, particularly from tuberculosis which was a rampant killer at the time, and 'bad feelings' also infected her state of mind. Lyndall Gordon has recently argued that the nature of her illness was epilepsy, which was kept secret out of a sense of shame. The truth is that we do not have a precise diagnosis for what was 'wrong' with Emily, although all theories hold some interest. In one case in particular she suffered what seems to have been a depressive episode following the death of a local friend, Sophia Holland, in 1844, which we will also consider in more detail later. Yet despite these disruptions, Emily found her time as a child and as an adolescent at the Amherst Academy invigorating, intellectually challenging and emotionally sustaining.

Emily's education did not end when she left Amherst Academy. She was to benefit from one more year at school, this time in a setting away from home. The majority of Emily's friends, including all of her gang of 'five', left Amherst Academy before Emily did. They had moved on to all-female boarding seminaries, perhaps because their parents considered that the local Academy was relatively inexperienced in its teaching of women. It may have been Emily's vulnerable health that had discouraged Edward from sending her to another establishment earlier, but in 1846 it was decided that his precocious daughter was sufficiently robust to risk a significant stint away from home. She was to attend an establishment nine miles out of Amherst. Emily wrote with excitement to Abiah on 26th June of that year:

> *I am fitting to go to South Hadley Seminary, and expect if my health is good to enter that institution a year from next fall. Are you not astonished to hear such news? You cannot imagine how much I am anticipating in entering there. It has been in my thought by day, and my dreams by night... I fear I am anticipating too much, and that some freak of fortune may overturn all my airy schemes for future happiness. But it is my nature always to anticipate more than I realize.*

The heady letter written to her friend to announce her news shows that at this stage Emily keenly anticipates life away from home, and imagines an ambitious if vague future, with a sense of premonition that all may not be as she best hopes.

One might imagine that leaving home, as Emily did on 30th September 1847, aged sixteen, would have been a source of extreme anxiety to the poet who later became so reclusive. Yet perhaps surprisingly, she seems to have settled in almost immediately. Teachers, as they had been at Amherst, were a source of immense comfort. She wrote to Austin, soon after arriving:

> *I went to see Miss Fiske. in her room yesterday & she read me, her letter from Sam & a right merry letter it was too... I love Miss. Fiske. very much & think I shall love all the teachers, when I become better acquainted with them & find out their ways, which I can assure you are almost "past finding out".*

Mount Holyoke Female Seminary had been founded by Mary Lyon, a devout visionary and a friend of Emily's inspirational geology teacher, Edward Hitchcock. The school's mission was to educate women at a time when many still thought women should not be educated. It was heavily influenced by fundamentalist thinking, as it had to rely financially on the support of evangelicals. One of these, for example – Hannah Porter – had created a Female Praying Circle, an influential secretive group, one of many designed to convert women to a form of fundamentalist Calvinism. The number of these 'circles' was on the rise, as a conservative reaction to the growing softer form of the faith, Unitarianism. It should be stressed that throughout her life, until her withdrawal (and a contributing factor to her giving up on society perhaps), Emily was subjected to the influence of many 'revivals': organised meetings and concerted efforts designed to convert people to Christ. These had happened more than once when she was in Amherst, but the influence would have been more sustained and pervasive at Mount Holyoke in South Hadley. The institutionalised effort to convert her, and others, would have bordered on the relentless. Even though as we shall see this was to cause her not a little confusion and pain, Emily never converted. This remained true even when she lost the other members of her family to the faith; a source of increased loneliness and intellectual alienation. It is reported that in some years not a single girl left South Hadley without having undergone a religious conversion. Emily's group held out more strongly, yet the figures still speak for themselves: in her year of some 250 girls, only around thirty left without giving in to Christ. Emily's fortitude in resisting the general religious sway is one reason modern readers identify with her, and admire her.

Emily was put to share a room with an orphaned first cousin, Emily Norcross, who had been brought up under the successive guardianships of her grandfather Joel and her uncle Albert Norcross. Cousin Emily was among those who had experienced a conversion to 'trust in the Saviour' a year before. Despite her religious proclivities, Emily found her 'an excellent room-mate' who did 'all in her power to make me happy'. Yet nothing could have matched the old gang at home. She tells Abiah on 6th November 1847:

> *When I left home, I did not think I should find a companion or a dear friend in all the multitude. I expected to find rough & uncultivated manners, & to be sure, I have found some of that stamp, but on the whole, there is an ease & grace a desire to make one another happy, which delights & at the same time, surprises me very much.*

She concludes that, 'I find no Abby. or Abiah. or Mary, but I love many of the girls.'

At a school for women, teachers would not have been trained to the standard expected for men, and Emily would not have encountered the academic rigour found at Yale or Harvard. Nonetheless, she was anxious about failing, as she had been at Amherst. Yet anxiety about academic success often comes hand in hand with high ability, and she was by all accounts an exemplary student – bright, dutiful and appreciative of committed teaching. We know she studied chemistry, physiology, calisthenics and singing, and that she practised the piano daily. She did no more Latin, which suggests that she had already translated four books of Virgil, the requirement needed for becoming a senior.

At Holyoke, Emily's days were highly regimented, which might have been a factor that made being there more manageable than one might expect for a young woman of excitable and sometimes nervous disposition and tendencies. A sample day is provided for Abiah. It gives a distinct flavour of how her time was spent:

> *At 6. o'clock, we all rise. We breakfast at 7. Our study hours begin at 8. At 9. we all meet in Seminary Hall, for devotions. At 10 ¼ I recite a review of Ancient History, in connection with which we read Goldsmith Grimshaw. At .11. I recite a lesson in "Pope's Essay on Man" which is merely transposition. At .12. I practice Calisthenics & at 12 ¼ read until dinner, which is at 12 ½ & after dinner, from 1 ½ until 2 I sing in Seminary Hall. From 2 ¾ until 3 ¾ I practise upon the Piano. At 3 ? I go to Sections, where we give in all our accounts for the day, including, Absence – Tardiness – Communications – Breaking Silent Study Hours – Receiving Company in our rooms & ten thousand other things... At 4½. we go into Seminary Hall, & receive advice from Miss. Lyon in the form of a lecture. We have Supper at 6. & silent-study hours from then until the retiring bell, which rings at 8 ¾, but the tardy bell does not ring until 9 ¾, so that we dont often obey the first warning to retire.*

It does not seem as if Pope's 'Essay on Man' was inspiring to Emily in the form it was taught here, yet the day was full and lively, with singing and piano playing regularly on the timetable. Emily was a proficient piano player, and when Edward had bought a piano for the Homestead in 1845 his daughter had been ecstatic. In addition to the above regime, a degree of domestic work was undertaken to help keep the fees down. We understand that in Emily's case this consisted of taking knives to the kitchen and washing them.

Politics and affairs pertaining to the outside world, however, were not much on the syllabus. Emily wrote to her brother on 21st October 1847:

> *Wont you please to tell me when you answer my letter who the candidate for President is? I have been trying to find out ever since I came here & have not yet succeeded. I dont know anything more about affairs in the world, than if I was in a trance... Do you know of any nation about to besiege South Hadley? If so, do inform me of it, for I would be glad of a chance to escape, if we are to be stormed. I suppose Miss Lyon. would furnish us all with daggers & order us to fight for our lives, in case such perils should befall us.*

Lack of thorough education on the subject, no doubt still felt inappropriate for women, may explain in part why later she was unable to engage with detail on the civil war, addressing it only in ways that some admirers find lacking. She wrote years later, in February 1863, to Higginson, who was an active campaigner on behalf of the freedom of slaves, and went to head up a Negro regiment, 'War feels to me an oblique place –'

Though Emily enjoyed South Hadley, home remained idyllic. A letter of 17th January 1848 to Abiah gives a striking account of her homecoming for Christmas a month earlier. This letter provides a rare sentimental picture of her mother, which belies the more remote image Emily liked to portray, at least showing that there was no fixed patterning in Emily's mind about how she experienced her.

> *Never did Amherst look more lovely to me & gratitude rose in my heart to God, for granting me such a safe return to my* OWN DEAR

*HOME. Soon the carriage stopped in front of our own house & all were at the door to welcome the returned one, from Mother with tears in her eyes down to Pussy... Oh! Abiah, it was the first meeting as it had been the first separation & it was a joyful one to all of us.*

Joyful to be reconnected with those at home, she was not yet ready to return for good. Emily settled back in at the seminary and when she became ill with a bad cough soon after Christmas, she did not write to tell her parents she was unwell, as she told Abiah in a letter of 16th May 1848; 'lest the folks should take me home'. She reveals some horror of the small town and domestic claustrophobia, and explains, again to Abiah, that she 'could not bear to leave teachers and companions before the close of term and go home to be dosed and receive the physician daily, and take warm drinks and be condoled with on the state of health in general by all the old ladies in town.' Emily's family heard about her being unwell, however, and Austin appeared suddenly to take her home, against her will.

It may have been this recurrence of her cough that caused Edward to decide that at the end of that school year, despite rumination about her continuing with her education for longer, Emily return from the seminary and never continue her formal studies. Thereafter she would look to be educated by her reading, and by a series of friends and informal tutors, some 'masters' – and turn herself into a writer.

## *The Soul selects her own Society* – Young adulthood

When Emily came home in the summer of 1848, aged seventeen, after the best part of a year at boarding school, life in Amherst was at first scintillating. She fell in with some old friends, and fast made many new ones. Her beloved childhood playmate Jane Humphrey was back in Amherst, now teaching at Amherst Academy, and when Abiah came back for a week in January 1850 they reconnected. There were others too, including Emily Fowler, who six years after Emily Dickinson's death wrote a poem about her friend's seclusion. Emily Fowler was four years older than Emily, cultured and beautiful, and considered by some to be the real belle of Amherst. Vinnie was away at a female seminary in Ipswich, also in Massachusetts, but despite missing her sister Emily found, as she wrote to Jane humphrey on 23rd January 1850, that Amherst had 'a good deal going on' and was 'full to the brim of fun'.

Emily also developed relationships with young men, such as her cousin William Cowper Dickinson with whom she had an exchange about a 'patronising' valentine of his; George Henry Gould, who is rumoured to have proposed to her; and Ben Newton. We will return to Gould, but it is important first to give Newton his due. A highly intelligent young man, Ben had been an apprentice and houseguest of Edward, much as Joseph Lyman had been. Nine years older than Emily, refreshingly, he was not orthodox. He was a liberal Unitarian and made a big impression on the still-developing girl, doing much to help her continue with an education after her time in South Hadley had come to an end. Writing about him in a tribute sent to his minister, the Reverend Mr Edward Everett Hale, a year after his early death from tuberculosis only a few years later in 1854, Emily said:

> *I was then but a child, yet I was old enough to admire the strength, and grace, of an intellect far surpassing my own, and it taught me many lessons, for which I thank it humbly, now that it is gone. Mr. Newton became to me a gentle, yet grave Preceptor, teaching me what to read, what authors to admire, what was most grand or beautiful in nature, and that sublimer lesson, a faith in things unseen, and in a life again, nobler and much more blessed –*
>
> *Of all these things he spoke – he taught me of them all, earnestly, tenderly, and when he went from us, it was as an elder brother, loved indeed very much, and mourned, and remembered.*

It is thought that a comment made later to Higginson referred to Newton: 'When a little Girl, I had a friend, who taught me Immortality – but venturing too near, himself – he never returned –' In Unitarianism, as opposed to Calvinism, giving up to 'things unseen' did not mean a cataclysmic giving up, but rather having faith in the mind by bestowing respectful attention on what is 'grand or beautiful' in nature or books; a belief that the mind can be gently taught to trust to ascend to what is beyond nature.

Newton sent Emily a copy of Emerson's poems, a book that may have had a liberating effect on her. Ralph Waldo Emerson (1803–82) was one of America's greatest poets, philosophers and essayists and it is worth dwelling on his influence for a flavour of the wider intellectual environment Emily would have been exposed to. In a memoir about her aunt published in 1932, Martha Dickinson Bianchi comments by means of apology for her lack of religious orthodoxy that, 'Emily, like others of her period, was involved in the conflict of old and new ideas in New England much to blame for our non-conforming spirits,' and makes reference to Emerson's mother, who tried to hold on to the faith of the past 'with both hands, yet all the time she doubted it'.

In a seminal poem of 1863, Emily makes one of the boldest and most beautifully articulated, philosophically argued 'statements' about one of the ways in which she views the human mind, and its relationship with God. It is worth citing in full, as it reveals a preoccupation with the strength and capacity of the human brain, a subject she is to return to again and again.

*The Brain – is wider than the Sky –*
*For – put them side by side –*
*The one the other will contain*
*With ease – and You – beside –*

*The Brain is deeper than the sea –*
*For – hold them – Blue to Blue –*
*The one the other will absorb –*
*As Sponges – Buckets – do –*

*The Brain is just the weight of God –*
*For – Heft them – Pound for Pound –*
*And they will differ – if they do –*
*As Syllable from Sound –*

Significantly, the poet finds the human brain 'just the weight of God' – acknowledging that in her view in that mood at least, God was the brain's creation and not the other way round, and therefore of exact equal weight: it is impossible to separate our experience of God from our own minds. The influential exponent of tangential views, Emerson, was also born in Boston and educated at Harvard. His first calling was to become a pastor, but he gave up this vocation shortly after the death of his first wife, because he felt unable to believe in the sacrament of the Lord's Supper. In 1833 Emerson visited England, where he met the Romantic poets Coleridge and Wordsworth, among others. Emerson brought back something of the Romantic spirit, and returned to America full of new ideas. In order to transmit these he worked assiduously as a lecturer, influencing many and evolving the quasi-religious concept of transcendentalism. He wrote several key essays, including 'Nature' (1836), in which he said, 'Nature is the incarnation of a thought... The world is mind precipitated,' and 'The Poet' (1844) in which he urges American poets to action, to forge the new land into original work. For the independent, creative mind all things were possible. Many, including writers such as Emily's great contemporary Walt Whitman, were directly influenced by Emersonian thought.

Although Emily never read Whitman, hearing that he was 'disgraceful', by which she means sexually shocking, the two have much in common, despite manifest differences in form and content: a mental courage, a radical experimentalism and religious unconventionality. Whitman's style, more free and lyrical than Emily's, although arguably less sharp linguistically, led him to write in 'Song of Myself':

*The pleasures of heaven are with me and the pains of*
*hell are with me,*
*The first I graft and increase upon myself, the latter*
*I translate into a new tongue.*

This could almost have become a mantra for Emily herself. The time was ripe for pioneering American men and women to begin to think for themselves. Emily may have been withdrawing socially, but she quickly absorbed lessons taught by friends such as Newton, and was keenly attuned to the main philosophical trends of the day. Those she selected as friends, throughout her life, even and perhaps particularly in solitude, included intellectuals against whose minds she could continue to try to sharpen her own. As she famously wrote in 1862:

> *The Soul selects her own Society –*
> *Then – shuts the Door –*

It seems that Newton also knew about her writing, and believed in her, for she adds in her note to Higginson, 'My dying Tutor told me that he would like to live till I had been a poet.'

We are offered a snapshot of Emily's relationship to a different young man in a letter to Abiah, written on 7th and 17th May 1850, a couple of years after her return home. Vinnie is still away at school, their mother is ill with neuralgia, and Emily struggling with domesticity and cooking, saying, 'I have always neglected the culinary arts, but attend to them now from necessity'. She writes about a young man who had come, interrupting her as she did the washing-up, wanting a 'ride in the woods' with her:

> *... I heard a well-known rap, and a friend I love* so *dearly came and asked me to ride in the woods... and I wanted to exceedingly – I told him I could not go, and he said he was disappointed – he wanted me very much – then the tears came into my eyes, tho' I tried to choke them back, and he said I* could, *and* should *go, and it seemed to me unjust. Oh I struggled with great temptation, and it cost me much of denial, but I think in the end I conquered... a kind of helpless victory...*

It is thought that this young caller might have been George Gould, of whom more later, but this passage is valuable in that it is one of the very few found in Emily's writing that seems to express real disappointment at the failure of a heterosexual tryst. It has often been observed that Emily's feelings for women seem more real and passionate than those she expresses for men. Even at this young age, nineteen, she seems to anticipate instead of marriage an increasing solitude and darkness. Later in the same letter, she expresses horror at the domestic:

> *What shall we do my darling, when trial grows more, and more, when the dim, lone light expires, and it's dark, so very dark,...*
> *... Mother is still an invalid tho' a partially restored one – Father and Austin still clamor for food, and I, like a martyr am feeding them. Would'nt you love to see me in these bonds of great despair, looking around my kitchen, and praying for kind deliverance... God keep me from what they call* households...

Perhaps it was in part her horror of 'households' that contributed to Emily's not being attracted to a married life. It is evident from her literary output, which was to begin in earnest before long, that during all the years she was at school and learning, a more troubled Emily was brewing. Also emerging was a writer who identified most closely less and less with those she met in her social network, but increasingly with other writers whose work she read, and whose characters spoke to her. As she put it later to Joseph Lyman, she considered the 'strongest friends of the soul – *books*'.

As time went by in Amherst, friends dispersed through marriage or work. For Emily this process of loss caused anxiety and distress, as she herself could no longer imagine a life beyond the home to which she was becoming increasingly tied. It does seem as if the next stage of development proved a stumbling block to her: 'how to grow up,' she wrote to Austin in a letter of 12th April 1853, 'I dont know.'

## *This is my letter to the World*
## The future artist practises her craft

*In Ebon Box, when years have flown*
*To reverently peer –*
*Wiping away the velvet dust*
*Summers have sprinkled there!*

*To hold a letter to the light –*
*Grown Tawny – now – with time –*
*To con the faded syllables*
*That quickened us like Wine!*

Letters, which were in time to become Emily's only method of communicating with those she loved, were even now of particular importance to the poet. In the verses above, which open a poem of 1860, she seems to show a prescient sense of how important her own correspondence might become to future generations, and to foreshadow the finding of her own cache of work after her death. In 1885 a brief two-line poem ran:

*A Letter is a joy of Earth –*
*It is denied the Gods –*

... and in June 1869 she wrote to Higginson, a sentiment echoed almost exactly to James D. Clark in 1882, 'A Letter always feels to me like immortality because it is the mind alone without corporeal friend.' Increasingly significant as she withdrew from face-to-face encounters, letters enabled her to be more herself than she felt she could be in the flesh.

Somewhere between school and her early twenties, Emily must have begun to write poetry, although the first work of which we have record is not dated until 1850. Certainly, the writing of letters from an early age (the first we have was written when she was eleven) helped shape the artist. As her poetic craft developed, correspondence continued to play a vital role not only in communicating in prose, but also in building a private readership for her poetry. We have on record only an estimated tenth of the letters she might have sent, yet this forms a large body of writing, and along with these letters were often included poems, variant versions of poems and fragments. It is as if, as time went by, the poems and the letters best represented her real persona, baffling as that might have been on occasion to the recipient, who must have struggled to follow the elliptical, sometimes lofty, sometimes tortured, meanings within. We have seen how at school Emily excelled in lively composition, witty and captivating, creating envy among some of her peers. The first piece of writing that we have of Emily's was prose, in the form of a letter written in 1842, when the poet was eleven, to her brother Austin who had left home to attend for a month a new, state-of-the-art academy, Williston Seminary in western Massachusetts. In the letter, we are introduced to Emily's lively mind, highly engaged manner of writing and sense of humour. Moreover, she employs no punctuation whatsoever, other than the odd dash. It is almost as if her mind is working too fast to bother with punctuation. As a mature writer, she continued to show the workings of her mind through her unusual grammar. No other is as eccentric as this, but in all cases it is as if the original syntax is there to show us that the mind is working as it goes, and encouraging us to break new ground in thought by refusing to tie it down to too tight a grammatical structure which, she suggests by her usage, suppresses original thinking.

*18 April 1842*

*My dear Brother*

*As Father was going to Northampton and thought of coming over to see you I thought I would improve the opportunity and write you a few lines – We miss you very much indeed you cannot think how odd it seems without you there was always such a Hurrah wherever you was I miss My bedfellow very much for it is rare that I can get any now for Aunt Elisabeth is afraid to sleep alone and Vinnie has to sleep with her but I have the privilege of looking under the bed every night which I improve as you may suppose the Hens get along nicely the chickens grow very fast I am afraid they will be so large that you cannot perceive them with the naked Eye...*

She rushes on, about 'the temperance dinner' that 'went off very well', about how 'Mr Jones has found in looking at his policy that his insurance is 8 thousand dollars instead of 6 which makes him feel a great deal better than he did at first,' and so on. Immediately, we feel the punch of her irrepressible personality when she commits herself to the page. One feels she must have experienced the same thrill she identified years later when she told Abiah that she found her own school composition 'exceedingly edifying'.

We have already seen extracts from several letters written to Abiah, the friend to whom she confessed the most in her late teens and early twenties. Abiah left Amherst as early as 1845, when Emily was fifteen, to go to another school. We have noted how much of Emily is revealed through this correspondence. It is significant that Abiah's absence fostered passionate connection through writing (most unlike the separation from her mother, who hated to put pen to paper), and when that absence was prolonged without comfort of reply, as we shall later see, Emily expresses anger and despair. This trend is repeated with various correspondents, for example Austin and Susan Gilbert, and from a psychological point of view reveals more of the Emily that was beset by anxiety than the Emily that was happy at school, or in rapture at a sunset. In an extraordinary composition of 11th January 1850, in which it is clear that she is enormously enjoying her powers of baroque articulation, she writes a long letter to her uncle, Joel Warren Norcross, which contains an extended passage about a fake dream she has had about how her uncle is suffering the tortures of hell for failing to fulfill the promise he had made of writing to her. 'You villain without a rival – unparraleled doer of crimes – scoundrel unheard of before – disturber of public peace – "creation's blot and blank"', she calls him. Although she is playful, we see both her capacity to feel hurt and neglected, and also the influence of the violent language of Calvinism to which she was subjected in some of her childhood reading, and from the pulpit and praying circles.

We also see in the letters that Emily begins to fear, in young adulthood, that she is developing in a direction different from the general trend. She is also displaying the volatility that was so important to the poet's make-up: the borderingly manic highs and lows, the vicissitudes of which can be difficult to track. Perhaps the practice of writing letters, and later poetry, helped her both to exorcise and to keep a frame on her own emotions.

Before we explore more of what was going on for her as a young woman, it is worth returning to a letter to Abiah of 28th March 1846 in which she gives an account of how she reacted to an early death, that of a friend aged fifteen, Sophia Holland, on 28th March 1844. It was following the shock of this loss caused by typhus that Emily had a prolonged period away from school. This is the first indicator that Emily could react more extremely than most to loss.

> *I have never lost but one friend near my age & with whom my thoughts & her own were the same. It was before you came to Amherst. My friend was Sophia Holland. She was too lovely for earth & she was transplanted from earth to heaven. I visited her often in sickness & watched over her bed. But at length Reason fled*

*and the physician forbid any but the nurse go into her room. Then it seemed to me I should die too if I could not be permitted to watch over her or even to look at her face. At length the doctor said she must die & allowed me to look at her a moment through the open door. I took off my shoes and stole softly to the sick room.*

*There she lay mild & beautiful as in health & her pale features lit up with an unearthly – smile. I looked as long as friends would permit & when they told me I must look no longer I let them lead me away. I shed no tear, for my heart was too full to weep, but after she was laid in her coffin & I felt I could not call her back again I gave way to a fixed melancholy.*

*I told no one the cause of my grief, though it was gnawing at my very heart strings. I was not well & I went to Boston & stayed a month & my health improved so that my spirits were better.*

Although the letter is less brilliant than many of Emily's, the language being more traditionally sentimental in the Victorian style, the fact that she herself links the death to the 'fixed melancholy' and not being well intimates a childhood depression. Indeed, we know that her father, despairing of her improving at home, sent her in May 1844 to stay with Aunt Lavinia in Boston for several weeks. This was the same aunt to whom Emily had gone as a toddler, and to whom she remained close throughout her life. This stint away helped to cheer the thirteen-year-old's spirits, as more lively letters sent back to Amherst from the young Emily testify.

Death, however, continued to preoccupy Emily, to what some might consider a morbid degree. In the nineteenth century of course early deaths, from tuberculosis in particular, but also scarlet fever and other conditions for which we have since found cures, affected many. Religious sermons that dwelt inevitably on death and the afterlife would have made it impossible for anybody not to think about this subject a good deal. The second home Emily moved to, when she was nine, was next to a cemetery, a fact that some think only compounded Emily's sensitivity about such matters. Although death was a common preoccupation and occurrence, Emily, as we are beginning to see, took things to extremes. Questions about what happens to us when we die become major themes in her poems. As an example, in a rueful, religiously satirical, painful work she says:

*I shall know why – when Time is over –*
*And I have ceased to wonder why –*
*Christ will explain each separate anguish*
*In the fair schoolroom of the sky –*

*He will tell me what "Peter" promised –*
*And I – for wonder at his woe –*
*I shall forget the drop of anguish*
*That scalds me now – that scalds me now!*

In other works, as if trying to master fear of death, or reliving an experience of a living death that some think she suffered during a later breakdown, and of which there is much evidence in the poetry, she rehearses, enacts and reenacts her own death. A sublime example of this is the wittily surreal and moving:

*I heard a Fly buzz – when I died –*
*The Stillness in the Room*
*Was like the Stillness in the Air –*
*Between the Heaves of Storm –*

*The Eyes around – had wrung them dry –*
*And Breaths were gathering firm*
*For that last Onset – when the King*
*Be witnessed – in the Room –*

*I willed my Keepsakes – Signed away*
*What portion of me be*
*Assignable – and then it was*
*There interposed a Fly –*

*With Blue – uncertain – stumbling Buzz –*
*Between the light – and me –*
*And then the Windows failed – and then*
*I could not see to see –*

Worrying about death would have provoked all the more anxiety given that Emily could not bring herself to accept what she viewed as the easy consolation of a Christian heaven. Earlier in the same letter of 28th March 1846 about Sophia Holland's death, written when Emily was just fifteen, Emily congratulates Abiah for her decision to convert, 'in favor of Christ'. She is, however, worried for herself, as she cannot find the same conviction within herself: 'I feel that I am sailing upon the brink of an awful precipice, from which I cannot escape & over which I fear my tiny boat will soon glide if I do not receive help from above. There is now a revival in College & many hearts have given way to the claims of God.'

A further letter to Abiah, of late 1850, voices an increasingly typical complaint of loneliness, actual and spiritual. The young Leonard Humphrey, from Amherst Academy, has died. He is the 'master' referred to below.

*I write Abiah to-night, because it is cool and quiet, and I can forget the toil and care of the feverish day, and then I am* selfish *too, because I am feeling lonely; some of my friends are gone, and some of my friends are sleeping – sleeping the churchyard sleep – the hour of evening is sad – it was once my study hour – my master has gone to rest, and the open leaf of the book, and the scholar at school* alone, *make the tears come, and I cannot brush them away; I would not if I could, for they are the only tribute I can pay the departed Humphrey…*

*To those bereaved so often that home is no more here, and whose communion with friends is had only in prayers, there must be much to hope for, but when the unreconciled spirit has nothing left but God, that spirit is lone indeed.*

Emily is the 'unreconciled' spirit, afraid yet also excited by her rebelliousness. Later in the same letter she continues on this theme:

> *... You are growing wiser than I am, and nipping in the bud fancies which I let blossom – perchance to bear no fruit, or if plucked, I may find it bitter. The shore is safer, Abiah, but I love to buffet the sea – I can count the bitter wrecks here in these pleasant waters, and hear the murmuring winds, but oh, I love the danger! You are learning control and firmness. Christ Jesus will love you more. I'm afraid he don't love me* any*!...*
>
> *I see but little of Abby;... She is more of a woman than I am, for I love so to be a child...*

The letters show us both that Emily is becoming a writer of great skill, employing rhetorical devices learned at school, sharp and satirical wit and a dexterous application of vocabulary, and also that she is growing apart from her contemporaries in other key ways; while they show signs of conformity, she, by then nineteen or twenty, still loves 'to be a child'. While they convert, she is letting rebellious 'fancies' blossom and loving the danger.

# I... never consciously touch a paint, mixed by another person – Literary Influences

One 'danger' Emily loved was reading. An anecdote that was recorded by Higginson on behalf of his wife when he visited Emily in 1870 runs thus:

> *Her father was not severe I should think but remote. He did not wish them to read anything but the Bible. One day her brother brought home Kavanagh hid it under the piano cover & made signs to her & they read it: her father at last found it was displeased... a student of his was amazed that they had never heard of Mrs. Child* [a popular contemporary novelist] *& used to bring them books & hide in a bush by the door. They were then little things in short dresses with their feet on the rungs of the chair. After the first book she thought in ecstasy "This then is a book! And there are more of them!"*

Hyperbolic as much of her communication was with Higginson, this story gives us a fascinating insight into the home life of the Dickinsons and into Emily's relationship with reading and books. Books to Emily were intoxicating, perhaps because they offered a clandestine pleasure, beyond the desired remit of her stern father; a secret key to an internal world that could help remove her from the restrictions of her circumstances, and from the less pleasurable aspects of her increasingly nervous personality. In addition, it should be pointed out that the influence of the Bible (not in fact the only reading matter her father allowed) did not have a negative impact on her poetry and correspondence. Indeed, it has been observed that she cites the Bible, if often satirically, more than any other text. Her poetry is profoundly infused with it both stylistically and in terms of its content. One way of looking at her body of poetic work is to see it as an idiosyncratic and courageous philosophical debate with the central purports of the Bible.

In a letter to Higginson of August 1862, she states that she would 'never consciously touch a paint, mixed by another person –'. By this she means that she is not aware of being derivative in any way. Yet for all her fierce originality, she was not without other key influences – and these helped to breathe life into her developing inspirations.

The Dickinson family subscribed to several major literary journals of their day, namely *The Atlantic Monthly*, *Harper's New Monthly Magazine*, *Scribner's Monthly* and *The Springfield Republican*, all of which published occasional fiction, poetry and literary criticism. Indeed, Emily was friends with Samuel Bowles, editor of *The Springfield Republican*, and with Josiah Gilbert Holland who associated with Bowles to create *Scribner's Monthly*. She tells Higginson how a story, 'Circumstance' by Harriet Prescott [Spofford], which she read in the May 1860 edition of *The Atlantic Monthly*, 'followed me in the Dark – so I avoided her –'. These publications would have kept her up to date with literary thinking, and introduced her to her important literary confidant, Higginson.

Exactly how Emily turned herself from exuberant letter-writer into poet is unclear, but certainly the intensity with which she absorbed books and other reading was part of that process. As a pupil, Emily would have encountered Milton, Alexander Pope, Virgil and many other writers chosen by the curriculum. No doubt much of this excited and pleased her, but we have little record of exactly what reading at school inspired her in particular. What we do know about what she read comes through comments in her letters, and while several of the works she refers to are what we might now consider great pieces of literature (for example, *Jane Eyre*, *Middlemarch*, *David Copperfield* and Emily Brontë's poems), many others were not. Commentators have noted that Emily seemed extremely broadminded in her reading for someone who was so ambitious a poet. Sentimental literature and poor poetry, as well as serious work, seem to have caught her attention. Sewall points out that there was no method in her reading, and of course it may well have been this in part that kept her own work so fresh.

Those books that she did read and love, she absorbed passionately. In some cases it appears as if her identification with books and their characters was as intense as her identification with real people – if not more intense as time went by.

We can't cover everything that she read, and there are excellent accounts of her eclectic reading matter in both Sewall and Habegger, but to give a flavour and to point out the most significant works, we will also consider the influences that seem to be the most present in her letters, poetry, and the way she lived her life.

*Kavanagh*, the novel she mentioned to Higginson as needing to be hidden under the piano cover, is a gentle exploration of New England life by Henry Wadsworth Longfellow. It was smuggled in to the house by brother Austin in 1849 when Emily was eighteen. The storyline in *Kavanagh* that seems to have fascinated her was one that concerned the account of a romantic friendship between two women, Alice and Cecilia, which Sewall argues becomes almost a model for her subsequent relations with Susan Gilbert, which we shall explore in depth later. The Dickinson copy of the text has Emily's pencil markings against several of the passages concerning this strand of the story. Another novel, *Picciola*, by X.B. Saintine, was also read in 1849. It was an international bestseller and told the story of the inner pilgrimage of the Count de Charney, who loses his faith and is imprisoned while conspiring against Napoleon. While imprisoned in a fortress called Fenestrella, Charney sees a small plant growing between paving stones, which becomes the vehicle by which he is able to recover his faith. Emily was given this book by cousin William Cowper Dickinson, probably in order to try to persuade her to believe more traditionally in God. Emily wrote to him, in the Valentine's Day letter of 1849, that she could see a real plant coming up within her own 'dungeon yard', 'the first living thing that has beguiled my solitude'. She goes on, 'It's a mysterious plant, & sometimes I fancy that it whispers pleasant things to me – of freedom – and the future.'

Typically, Emily interprets the image of the flower from the novel for her own ends. She makes of it not a religious instrument, but one that whispers to her, movingly, of 'freedom – and the future'.

Dickinson read *Jane Eyre* in 1849, in a copy lent to her by her father's colleague and family friend Elbridge Gridley Bowdoin. It absorbed her, even though she did not learn that it had been written by a woman until 1851. We have little record of her response to it, but she marked various passages, including a section about the sternly devout St John Rivers who discovers Jane Eyre in extremis when she has run away from Thornfield Hall, and later proposes to her. The passage Emily highlighted reads, 'The humanities and amenities of life had no attraction for him – its peaceful enjoyments no charm. Literally, he lived only to aspire –'. Commentators have thought that Emily might have had her increasingly remote father in mind when she marked this passage, but it is also possible that the description reminded her of herself. For her own aspiration was developing rapidly; she was becoming increasingly single-minded, with a tendency to find that most of the social world 'had no attraction' for her, like Rivers.

Further evidence of Dickinson's engagement with the text of *Jane Eyre* is that in the year she read it, she was given a dog by her father, perhaps partly to protect her. This was a Newfoundland, a particularly large breed. Emily and her enormous pet must have made a striking picture side by side. She called the dog Carlo: the name of St John Rivers' dog from Charlotte Brontë's most famous work.

There were some four hundred books in the Dickinson library, now housed at Harvard University, and it is difficult to know which Emily did or didn't read. Yet out of these a few more are known to have been important for her, among them Donald Grant Mitchell's cycle of essays, *Reveries of a Bachelor*, written under the pseudonym Ik Marvel. The book presents the memories and daydreams of a bachelor whose life is defined by a series of unconsummated desires. Emily wrote of this book's 'exquisite writing' and refers to it as a 'great book'; to her future sister-in-law Sue she writes in 1851, 'If you were only here – perhaps we would have a "Reverie" after the form of Ik Marvel.'

Habegger also makes an important contribution to Dickinson studies in arguing a strong case for the influence of the English novelist Dinah Mulock Craik, author of two novels, *The Head of the Family* and *Olive*, in which he sees many echoes of Emily's life. In particular, he observes the overt theme of a 'Master' in the life of one of Craik's characters, and the place of a 'terror' in another's. We shall come to see the significance for Emily of these words, in later chapters.

*Poems* by Currer, Ellis and Acton Bell, published in 1846, also struck a chord. We are not sure when Emily got hold of this publication of these pseudonymous poems of Emily, Anne and Charlotte Bronte, but we know how deeply she admired them: Susan Dickinson chose Emily Brontë's 'No Coward Soul is Mine' to be read at the poet's funeral. There was also a wildness in Emily Dickinson's literary spirit, which would have been encouraged in particular by Emily Brontë's emotional courage.

It seems that Emily came to Shakespeare relatively late. In 1851 we know from a diary that Vinnie kept that Emily occasionally attended a reading club at which the members read Shakespearean texts, but there is no evidence that Emily became passionately engaged with him at that time. England's great playwright is however referred to by Emily as being the first writer she consumed when her long eye treatment had come to an end, fourteen years later, in 1865. Then she writes of *Othello* and *Anthony and Cleopatra* in her letters, revealing deep interest in Shakespeare's exploration of passionate love. Significantly, she quotes Anthony's lines from the latter play in a key, late document written to Susan Gilbert.

The long, narrative poem *Aurora Leigh*, written by one of Emily's most influential contemporaries Elizabeth Barrett-Browning (1806–61), held a particular power. Emily read this work in 1859, at an important moment in her development, when she was becoming increasingly committed to dedicating her life to the work of becoming a poet. The poem concerns Aurora Leigh who rejects marriage on the grounds that, although a woman, she prefers to dedicate her life to art. Although Barrett-Browning did not herself shun marriage, famously wedding fellow poet Robert Browning in 1846, the subject of a woman's relationship to art is powerfully articulated and explored in this major work. Barrett-Browning writes Aurora's lines:

> *Because I love the beautiful, I must*
> *Love pleasure chiefly, and be overcharged*
> *For ease and whiteness! Well – you know the world*
> *And only miss your cousin; 'tis not much! –*
> *But learn this: I would rather take my part*
> *With God's Dead, who afford to walk in white…*

Emily herself famously began to wear white almost exclusively, a habit that grew alongside her tendency to withdraw from much of the world, and in the following mysterious, celebrated lines of hers, alongside many other references to the significance of the colour white, she shows a deep identification with Barrett-Browning's character:

*Mine – by the Right of the White Election!*
*Mine – by the Royal Seal!*
*Mine – by the sign in the Scarlet prison –*
*Bars – cannot conceal!*

*Mine – here – in Vision – and in Veto!*
*Mine – by the Grave's Repeal –*
*Titled – Confirmed –*
*Delirious Charter!*
*Mine – long as Ages steal!*

Barrett-Browning's work helped Emily commit to the path of becoming a poet. A beautiful poem, written about the younger poet's experience of reading the elder, testifies to how intimately she connected with other writers. It shows us that reading *Aurora Leigh* was experienced as a 'Conversion of the Mind', and how in it, she found a 'Divine Insanity' that would act as a magical antidote when she needed it:

*I think I was enchanted*
*When first a sombre Girl –*
*I read that Foreign Lady –*
*The Dark – felt beautiful –*

*And whether it was noon at night –*
*Or only Heaven – at noon –*
*For very Lunacy of Light*
*I had not power to tell –*

*The Bees – became as Butterflies –*
*The Butterflies – as Swans –*
*Approached – and spurned the narrow Grass –*
*And just the meanest Tunes*

*That Nature murmured to herself*
*To keep herself in Cheer –*
*I took for Giants – practising*
*Titanic Opera –*

*The Days – to Mighty Metres stept –*
*The Homeliest – adorned*
*As if unto a Jubilee*
*'Twere suddenly confirmed –*

*I could not have defined the change –*
*Conversion of the Mind*
*Like Sanctifying in the Soul –*
*Is witnessed – not explained –*

*'Twas a Divine Insanity –*
*The Danger to be sane*
*Should I again experience –*
*'Tis Antidote to turn –*

*To Tomes of Solid Witchcraft –*
*Magicians be asleep –*
*But Magic – hath an element*
*Like Deity – to keep –*

Other traceable influences were seventeenth-century stylists, such as Sir Thomas Browne and George Herbert. The hymns of Isaac Watts also played a major part in the development of her poetic voice, as did the influence of the American Plain Style and of Noah Webster and Lexicography. For more detail about these, along with a brilliant analysis of Emily Dickinson's grammar, see Cristanne Miller's *Emily Dickinson: A Poet's Grammar* (Harvard University Press, 1987).

The portrait of Edward as a father who disapproved of his daughters' reading echoes much of what we know about his fierceness and conservatism, albeit this was combined with parental concern and a belief that his girls should receive some education. It was widely believed at that period in both America and Britain that reading might give women ideas beyond their station. Behind this may have been a fear that it would open their eyes and cause them to abandon domestic roles much needed by the traditional institution of marriage; and also more magically, that reading might breed 'fancies' that might not be good for the mind. Edward's influence was, perhaps, so pervasive that Emily's entire literary life was conducted under cover, so to speak, in order not to gain the disapproval of her father, who expressed distaste for literary women. This may well have been the case, or part of the reason, that she shunned publication throughout her life.

## *Awake ye muses nine...*
## A Young Writer is Born

In April 1850, Emily wrote one of her most tantalisingly mysterious messages in a letter to Jane Humphrey, the woman who had shared her bed when staying with the Dickinsons as a girl, and who had recently been back in Amherst teaching at Amherst Academy. Emily's letters to Jane had remained loving and passionate. She confesses, 'I have dared to do strange things – bold things, and have asked no advice from any – I have heeded beautiful tempters, yet do not think I am wrong.'

Treating Jane as a confessor, as she had Abiah when she disclosed her religious doubts, Emily continues in a manner that may well have perplexed the recipient:

> *... it would relieve me to tell you all, to sit down at your feet, and look in your eyes, and confess what* you only *shall know, an experience bitter, and sweet, but the sweet did so beguile me – and life has had an aim, and the world has been too precious for your poor – and striving sister! The winter was all one dream, and the spring has not yet waked me, I would* always *sleep, and dream... What do you weave from all these threads, for I know you hav'nt been idle the while I've been speaking to you, bring it nearer the window, and I will see, it's all wrong unless it has one gold thread in it, a long, big shining fibre which hides the others – and which will fade away into Heaven while you hold it, and from there come back to me.*

The letter goes on, reaching mysterious fever pitch:

> *I hope belief is not wicked, and assurance, and perfect trust – and a kind of twilight feeling before the moon is seen – I hope human nature has truth in it – Oh I pray it may not deceive – confide – cherish, have a great faith in – do you dream from all this what I mean? Nobody* thinks *of the joy, nobody* guesses *it, to all appearance old things are engrossing, and new ones are not revealed, but there* now *is nothing old, things are budding, and springing, and singing, and you rather think you are in a green grove, and it's branches that go, and come. I shall see you* sometime *darling…*

Some have thought Emily must have been writing about a love affair, and 'bold things' be of a romantic nature – perhaps with a man, or because of the guilty nature of the secret, possibly with a woman. More likely, however, this is an ecstatic expression of the realisation that her own path lies with the Transcendentalist pursuit of poetry: the articulation to herself of her vocation, despite her gender. It comes almost as a religious conversion. It gives her life an 'aim' and is a 'bold' answer to the question of how to harness her intellect and passions. It is as secret as a love affair, because it involves a conscious rejection of conventional religion, in favour of the Emersonian view that 'human nature has truth in it'. It involves on many levels defying her powerful father.

It is surprising though, if poetic vocation is the subject of the above letter, that we only have one poem surviving from the year 1850 – and no others until 1852. Her correspondence during these years, however, as we have seen in the chapter 'This is my letter to the World', was becoming increasingly florid in style.

Her first recorded poem, oddly, takes the form of a relatively conventional Valentine poem sent to her father's law partner, Elbridge Bowdoin, a committed bachelor. Perhaps inspired by her reading of Ik Marvel's *Reveries of a Bachelor*, Emily sent him the work, which urges courtship and marriage, in playful mode.

When at Mount Holyoke, Emily had bemoaned to Austin the fact that she had not received a Valentine that year of 1848, and that, 'Probably, Mary, Abby & Viny have received scores of them from the infatuated wights in the neighborhood while your *highly accomplished gifted elder sister* is entirely overlooked.' In 1850 she decided she would be proactive on this front in the future, and thus minimise the risk of feeling neglected.

If we had only had this piece of juvenilia to go by, it is doubtful that anyone would have spied special genius in the lines. The poem has a traditional *aabb* rhyme scheme, and some of the lines seem overcrowded: in short, the work of an excited newcomer to the form. Starting by calling on the 'muses nine' to 'sing me a strain divine', the poem tells its recipient:

> *God hath made nothing single but* thee *in his world so fair!*
> *The* bride, *and then the* bridegroom, *the* two, *and then the* one,
> *Adam, and Eve, his consort, the moon, and then the sun;*
> *the life doth prove the precept, who obey shall happy be,*

And so on, building to a stranger, darker, more recognisably Dickinsonian sentiment:

> *The* worm *doth woo the* mortal, *death claims a living bride,*
> *night unto day is married, morn unto eventide;...*
> *thou art a* human *solo, a being cold, and lone,*
> *wilt have no kind companion, thou* reap'st *what thou hast* sown.
> *Hast never silent hours, and minutes all too long,*
> *and a deal of sad reflection, and* wailing *instead of song?*

The fact that this is a valentine concerned with the theme of matching pairs together to eradicate single entities is strikingly ironic in Emily's case. Was she aware that her song might become a wail? Or her wail of loneliness a poetic song?

Another, baroque creation, a prose 'Valentine', also dated 1850 and thought to have been sent to the brilliant but impoverished young man George Gould, was published anonymously in a student magazine, *The Indicator*. Gould, six foot eight, a close friend of Austin's, an excellent orator, an admirer of Emily's and rumoured even to have proposed to her, was at the time chairman of the editorial board of the new publication. Emily's spoof valentine, sent in with hoards of others by different authors, begins 'Sir, I desire an interview; meet me at sunrise, or sunset, or the new moon – the place is immaterial,' and goes on:

*Our friendship sir, shall endure till sun and moon shall wane no more, till stars shall set, and victims rise to grace the final sacrifice... I am Judith the heroine of the Apocrypha, and you the orator of Ephesus.*

*That's what they call a metaphor in our country. Don't be afraid of it, sir, it won't bite.*

Clearly, this was no common love letter – more a display of literary mastery. The comment written on it, probably by Gould's colleague Henry Shipley, was, 'I wish I knew who the author is. I think she must have some spell, by which she quickens the imagination, and causes the high blood "run frolic through the veins".'

It is not known how this work made its way into print, other than that it was selected as being the best of the valentines sent in that year. We do not know if Emily gave her permission or not, and Emily Fowler – apparently defending Dickinson – expressed annoyance that the writing had made its way to a public readership. It has been observed, however, that this may have been the one composition she had allowed to be published. Perhaps 'the beautiful tempters' of her letter to Jane Humphrey were the young editors of *The Indicator*, seeking her permission to publish? Perhaps, as Habegger muses, upon finding out about it, her father reprimanded her sternly, considering publication inappropriate for women and ever after circumventing publication even when Emily was directly asked for work? Instead, might it be that she chose to circulate her poems ever more widely in private letters, thus avoiding any accusation of being the kind of literary woman her own father may despise?

A rumour that Gould had proposed to Emily was started after the poet's death by Vinnie in the 1890s, and picked up in the 1920s by an early biographer, Genevieve Taggard, who based her book *The Life and Mind of Emily Dickinson* on this supposition. She broadcast the theory that Emily took to wearing white as a sign of eternal fidelity to Gould, her father having disapproved of the match on the grounds of the young man's lack of fortune. Yet this does not ring true, like most rumoured theories about Emily's life that proliferated after her death, not least because Emily did not adopt the habit of wearing white exclusively until many years later. It also seems unlikely that Edward would have disapproved of such a brilliant young man. Subsequent scholars believe that while Gould and Emily were clearly friends, and that he may have been the beau who called for a ride when Emily was washing dishes in the letter to Abiah of 1850, there is no evidence that Emily was in love with him, nor moreover that she ever wished to marry him. It is thought that Vinnie was seeking to give a single-cause explanation for her sister's eccentric habit of wearing white and withdrawing from the world. This may have been a smokescreen for other reasons she wished to cloak, such as an affair with the married Charles Wadsworth, or even with Sue. More likely Vinnie didn't know the reasons fully – and simply sought to protect her sister by giving a 'rational' explanation for behaviour that others had found increasingly strange.

To return to Emily's poetry: after the valentine couplets of 1850, we have only one poem from 1852 (another juvenile verse, the lively and bold 'Sic transit Gloria mundi / "how doth the busy bee") then in 1853 one more ('On this wondrous sea – sailing silently – / Ho! Pilot! Ho!') but it is not until 1858, when Emily is twenty-seven, that we begin to see poems in any quantity with marks of the originality for which Emily Dickinson became renowned.

Before we examine critical elements of the often painful journey that helped transform juvenilia into mature work, it is worth examining a second famous poem that looks back at Emily's childhood. This poem, written in 1862, speaks with high confidence of the gift she seems to have known from school days that she possessed. The present was given to her 'by the Gods', and the nature of it was not financial wealth, but the ability to make a bank for 'the mint' she caught: her investment was in 'the name of Gold' – i.e. the reputation she knew she could earn from her remarkable talent. This is a key poem, worth reading carefully. 'The Difference' was what made Emily bold.

*It was given to me by the Gods –*
*When I was a little Girl –*
*They give us Presents most – you know –*
*When we are new – and small.*
*I kept it in my Hand –*
*I never put it down –*
*I did not dare to eat – or sleep –*
*For fear it would be gone –*
*I heard such words as "Rich" –*
*When hurrying to school –*
*From lips at Corners of the Streets –*
*And wrestled with a smile.*
*Rich! 'Twas Myself – was rich –*
*To take the name of Gold –*
*And Gold to own – in solid Bars –*
*The Difference – made me bold –*

Emily had no financial independence. Unlike other great writers in America at that time, and most of her contemporaries, she did not work, nor, as far as we know, express a wish to work. One of the arguments put forward for the cause of her withdrawal from society was that she suffered from agoraphobia. We will consider her mental vulnerability later, but it is fascinating to note that agoraphobia means, literally, fear of the marketplace. If Emily feared the results of the marriage market, of ordinary trading, of public arenas more fit for 'frogs' as the metaphor has it in her famous, short poem about fame, 'I'm Nobody! Who are you?' ('How dreary – to be – Somebody!/How public – like a Frog –'), she was at the same time creating an internal investment system that would, later, set the markets alight. She would in time become the princess that the public kissed. Unable to leave home, and/or choosing to stay within the superior Dickinson compound as a conscious choice, Emily was taking a gamble of immense proportions: an experiment with her life, matched only by the experimentation in her poetry. Later she will write, again, about her relationship to ambition and to intimations of greatness. The gain may be posthumous, but paradoxically the victory would have been made this side of heaven. She would not yield to easy religious answers: the work would speak for itself.

*'Tis so much joy! 'Tis so much joy!*
*If I should fail, what poverty!*
*And yet, as poor as I,*
*Have ventured all opon a throw!*
*Have gained! Yes! Hesitated so –*
*This side the Victory!...*

*And if I gain! Oh Gun at sea,*
*Oh Bells, that in the steeples be!...*

## *To own a Susan of my own*
## Looking for love, troubles, and the refining of a vocation

Notwithstanding her growing belief in herself as a writer, there were other elements of Emily's life that were less satisfactory. Arguably it was difficulty in matters of love and growing up that drove the poet to sequester herself away, making her life increasingly focused on the vocation of being a poet. This vocation, at times, was to feel like martyrdom.

*The Martyr Poets – did not tell –*
*But wrought their Pang in syllable –*
*That when their mortal name be numb –*
*Their mortal fate – encourage Some –*

*The Martyr Painters – never spoke –*
*Bequeathing – rather – to their Work –*
*That when their conscious fingers cease –*
*Some seek in Art – the Art of Peace –*

This 'Martyr' poem is from her prolific period a few years later. Before her poetic genius could really be set on fire, it needed more of the petrol of love and life to be poured upon it: then a conflagration could occur.

The departure of her beloved gang of friends from Amherst created increasing panic and excessive sadness in Emily; as if she imagined they would have stayed forever as a magic circle, forever young, with her nervy brilliance near the centre. Instead, she found herself still at home tending to household duties and unmarried, albeit perhaps by desire as much as accident, and increasingly ambivalent and anxious about what others might view as normal social interaction.

She watched powerlessly as friends took husbands, or left to work, or for other reasons; some she chided, while at the same time wishing them luck; to a few she expressed deep anxiety. Being without her close group of local friends was not the future Emily had anticipated. Their taking up conventional lives seems to have surprised and scared her. She idealised home, while at the same time in reality often finding it depressing. In addition, she was losing others to religion, where she could not follow – even those closest to her at home. During the largest evangelical wave in her lifetime, in 1850, her sister Vinnie, her father and Sue all 'yielded to Christ'. In a few years Austin would follow them, leaving her, although still respected, spiritually stranded within the bosom of her own family. Emily had a void, which needed filling. It is important to take time in telling the next strand of the story, for it involves a character who was arguably the most important person in Emily's life and whose presence in the Dickinson family changed everything.

* * *

Susan Gilbert was born nine days after Emily Dickinson, some ten miles out of Amherst in Greenfield, Massachusetts on 19th December 1830, the youngest of seven siblings. Her mother had died of consumption when she was six and her father, a severe alcoholic, when she was eleven. Having been brought up with one of her sisters, Martha, by Sophia Van Vranken, a maternal aunt, in Geneva, New York, Susan moved with Martha in 1846 to Amherst to live with an older, married sister, Harriet Gilbert Cutler. There, Susan attended Amherst Academy between the years of 1846 and 1849, overlapping with Emily's presence there only briefly. From 1849–50, she was sent to the best girls' school available, Utica Female Seminary, west of Troy in the state of New York. Susan was reputed to be considered the 'quintessence of perfection' (as Martha reported) and of a brilliant mind. In the summer of 1850, catastrophe hit the Gilbert family when sister Mary Gilbert Learned died of puerperal fever while giving birth in Michigan. Martha had gone to help her sister, and did not return to Amherst until February 1851. Meanwhile, Susan was left in Amherst without Martha.

It was during this period of bereavement in early 1851 that Sue and Emily became friends. The poet's earliest recorded message to Susan was sent at the end of February of that year. At the same time as Emily was befriending Susan, Austin was also showing an interest. He asked Sue to ride with him just two weeks after Mary's death. When Austin went away to teach for a term in Sunderland, north of Amherst in Massachusetts that year, his missives to Susan multiplied. In his absence Susan visited the Dickinson household often, and became a firm favourite. When Austin returned for Thanksgiving in November, a romance between him and Susan began, which was conducted discreetly. Emily by all accounts remained unaware of the romance, and when in the autumn of 1851 Susan left Amherst and found a teaching job in Baltimore, Emily's own letters to Susan grow in number and intensity, alongside Austin's.

At the same time, Emily also writes to Austin often, telling him about the precious time she is spending with Martha and Susan. She chides him for being away, yet at the same time delights in the close attention of Susan and Martha. She seems in her element and happy, at the centre of a girlish clan. It is when Susan herself goes away that, through her letters, Emily begins to show an attachment more powerful than the ordinary, even by her own standards of intensity. The degree of anxiety and passionate need expressed to Susan speak of an admiration and longing for the woman herself, but also of a more general panic about feeling abandoned: a primitive panic, which as we have seen may have been sparked off in baby-hood.

We know that Emily had not picked up on the increasingly romantic (if not altogether smooth) nature of Susan's relationship with her brother, as in a letter of January 1852 she expresses deep fear at the thought that Susan and Martha might get married, but clearly not to Austin:

> *I have thought today of what would become of me when the "bold Dragon" shall bear you both away, to live in his high mountain – and leave me here alone; and I could have wept bitterly… and then Susie, I thought how these short adieus of our's might – Oh Sue, they* might *grow sadder and longer, and that bye and bye they would not be said any more, nor any more* forever, *for that of our precious band, some* one *should pass away.*

In another letter of April of the same year, largely full of rapture for Sue, Emily again brings up the subject of men, almost as if to test Susan's response. It is clear that Emily does not respond to men in the way she feels she ought, and that she admires in Susan an even more 'stone'-like quality than she herself possesses:

> *I do think it's wonderful, Susie, that our hearts dont break,* every day, *when I think of all the whiskers, and all the gallant men, but I guess I'm made with nothing but a hard heart of stone, for it dont break any, and dear Susie, if mine is stony, your's is stone, upon stone, for you never yield* any…

Although she brings up the question of men and marriage, she also notes that Susan is 'strangely silent upon that subject'. Sue's silence may have been the result of a desire to protect Emily from the reality of her relationship with Austin, who pursued her relentlessly with letters of almost as high a pitch as Emily's, or it may have been that Susan herself was, as she turned out to be, profoundly ambivalent about the subject of marriage. We do not have Susan's letters to Emily, bar one or two, and it is frustrating not to know to what degree Emily's feelings were reciprocated, although it is safe to assume that much of the intensity and 'spiritual relationship' (as it was later described by Austin) was, at least for a time and to some degree, shared. Yet we can see that Emily's feelings during the time of Sue's absence grow increasingly idealised and powerful, in a manner that may have bewildered the recipient. At the same time as she is writing to Austin, more practical letters full of information, yet also scolding him for his continuing absence (as if it were a crime not to be at home and to abandon her), she continues to write to Sue with what by now looks like passionate love, revealing again a dread of separation. In a letter of circa 6th February 1852, she writes:

> *Oh my darling one, how long you wander from me, how weary I grow of waiting and looking, and calling for you; sometimes I shut my eyes, and shut my heart towards you, and try hard to forget you because you grieve me so, but you'll never go away, Oh you never will – say, Susie, promise me again, and I will smile faintly – and take up my little cross again of sad –* sad *separation… Love always, and ever, and true!*

Also probably in February, she writes:

> *… Oh Susie, I would nestle close to your warm heart, and never hear the wind blow, or the storm beat, again. Is there any room there for me, or shall I wander away all homeless and alone? Thank you for loving me, darling, and* will *you "love me more if ever you come home"? – it is enough, dear Susie, I know I shall be satisfied. But what can I do towards you? –* dearer *you* cannot *be, for I love you so already, that it almost breaks my heart – perhaps I can love you* anew, *every day of my life, every morning and evening – Oh if you will let me, how happy I shall be!*

> *... Never mind the letter, Susie; you have so much to do; just write me every week* one line, *and let it be "Emily, I love you," and I will be satisfied!*

When Emily writes later on in February, there is a tone of serious pain and bewilderment at her own feelings, beyond the rhetorical, 'I do not know; in thinking of those I love, my reason is all gone from me, and I do fear sometimes that I must make a hospital for the hopelessly insane, and chain me up there such times, so I wont injure you.' Emily seems to have feared her own growing desire, to the point that she worried she might have to injure Susan out of a combination of need and confused intensity.

Another love letter of late April 1852 reaches fever pitch – with Emily telling Susan how when she was at church and the worthy pastor said, '"Our Heavenly Father," I said "Oh Darling Sue"; when he read the 100th Psalm, I kept saying your precious letter all over to myself'. This letter of Emily's also includes the following statement, 'You wont cry any more, will you, Susie, for my father will be your father, and my home will be your home, and where you go, I will go, and we will lie side by side in the kirkyard.' Here, Emily imagines them like a married couple, together forever underground.

In late June 1852, before Sue's return to Amherst, Emily writes, 'Why, Susie, it seems to me as if my absent Lover was coming home so soon – and my heart must be so busy, making ready for him.' Ironically, it was not of course Emily but Austin who married Susan Gilbert. Their engagement was confirmed in 1853.

Emily seems to have accepted the match. After all, she had little choice and Austin and Susan being tied would have meant that Susan would be perpetually bound to the Dickinson clan in the manner Emily had longed for. Yet while on the one hand accepting the situation, she continued to declare her need for Susan. In a letter of 12th March 1853, she writes, putting herself still very much at the centre of their drama:

*One thing is true, Darling, the world will be none the wider, for Emilie's omnipresence, and two big hearts will beat stouter, as tidings from* me *come in. I love the opportunity to serve those who are mine and to soften the least asperity in the path which ne'er "ran smooth...."*

Yet at the same time as offering her services to benefit their love affair, she goes on to declare that she cannot do without Sue a second longer and resorts to her worst tendency: emotional blackmail: '... your absence insanes me so – I do not feel so peaceful, when you are gone from me... Do you ever look homeward, Susie, and count the lonely hours Vinnie and I are spending, because that you are gone?'

It is true that letters between women of the Victorian period were often romantic in ways that would be considered sexualised today, but were not consciously so then. Yet most commentators agree that Emily's feelings for Sue were more than ordinarily florid and sentimental. Although Emily Dickinson could not know it, her letters to Susan closely resemble those written by Elizabeth Barrett-Browning to her clandestine lover, Robert Browning, before they eloped. Emily's letters to Susan have more in common with the language of longing and suppression – of volcanic repression and threatened explosiveness – exchanged between those two famous literary lovers than with the usually heightened exchanges between women of that time in history.

A different kind of letter, of 15th January 1854, is particularly significant, in that it shows us the degree of need Emily projected onto Susan. It involves a fantasy about Sue as protector and ideal mother, in a way that not only Sue, but no one could have matched up to. It also shows us a degree of psychic oddity, which informs our thinking about Emily's withdrawal and agoraphobic tendencies:

*I'm just from meeting, Susie, and as I sorely feared, my "life" was made a "victim." I walked – I ran – I turned precarious corners –*

*One moment I was not – then soared aloft like Phoenix, soon as the foe was by – and then anticipating an enemy again, my soiled and drooping plumage might have been seen emerging from just behind a fence, vainly endeavoring to fly once more from hence. I reached the steps… How big and broad the aisle seemed, full huge enough before, as I quaked slowly up – and reached my usual seat!*

*In vain I sought to hide behind your feathers – Susie – feathers and* Bird *had flown, and there I sat, and sighed, and wondered I was scared so, for surely in the whole world was nothing I need to fear – Yet there the Phantom was, and though I kept resolving to be as brave as Turks, and bold as Polar Bears, it did'nt help me any.*

This description of what appears to have been what is now known as a panic attack stands out among her correspondence. It shows the terrifying lack of perspective Emily's mind was capable of; a tendency often employed to brilliant effect in her poems to magnify the ordinary to become something grotesque. In this instance, it was an aisle that took on monstrous proportions. It was, after all, an aisle (albeit not the same one) down which Susan and her brother would walk, if not for another two years.

In late August 1854, possibly in need of respite from the Dickinson intensity, Sue went to stay in Geneva, New York, with the aunt who had brought her up. Relations with Austin were also the source of anxiety as well as pleasure, and Sue continued to show signs of uncertainty about the match and marriage. Austin's own passion was so intense that it continued to overrule Sue's distrust, although he also failed to notice much about what might have been happening internally to his beloved. Emily also, true to form, shows annoyance at the 'abandonment', rather than understanding her friend's own needs or preoccupations. She says sardonically, 'I do not miss you Susie – of course I do not miss you… Don't *feel* it – no – any more than the stone feels, that it is very cold …'

Susan's apparent stone-heartedness in the letter in which Emily discusses men is evidently not so admirable when perceived in relation to Emily herself, and the poet's own incapacity to have her heart broken by a man clearly does not apply to her relationship with her future sister-in-law.

Emily's articulation of helplessness and martyred pain must have made for uncomfortable reading on Sue's part. Continuing not to hear from her as regularly as she wished, in part perhaps because Susan did not know how to manage an ongoingly intense relationship with Emily at the same time as having one with Austin, Emily writes angrily in a letter dated 'about' 1854:

> *Sue – you can go or stay – There is but one alternative – We differ often lately, and this must be the last.*
>
> *You need not fear to leave me lest I should be alone, for I often part with things I fancy I have loved, – sometimes to the grave, and sometimes to an oblivion rather bitterer that death – thus my heart bleeds so frequently that I shant mind the hemorrhage, and I only add an agony to several previous ones, and at the end of the day remark – a bubble burst!*
>
> *Such incidents would grieve me when I was but a child, and perhaps I could have wept when little feet hard by mine, stood still in the coffin, but eyes grow dry sometimes, and hearts get crisp and cinder, and had as lief burn.*
>
> *Sue – I have lived by this. It is the lingering emblem of the Heaven I once dreamed, and though if this is taken, I shall remain alone, and though in that last day, the Jesus Christ you love, remark he does not know me – there is a darker spirit will not disown it's child.*
>
> *Few have been given me, if I love them so, that for* idolatory, *they are removed from me – I simply murmur* gone, *and the billow dies away into the boundless blue, and no one knows but me, that one went down today. We have walked very pleasantly – Perhaps this is the point at which out paths diverge – then pass on singing Sue, and up the distant hill I journey on.*

This extraordinary letter includes a poem. This was the first of many written to and about Sue, who proved a powerful muse for Emily. Arguably, it was passion for this relationship that acted as the springboard for her becoming a poet of stature. Susan was a personal and a literary inspiration throughout her life.

The poem starts:

*I have a Bird in spring*
*Which for myself doth sing –*

and concludes, self consolingly:

*Then will I not repine,*
*Knowing that Bird of mine*
*Though flown*
*Shall in a distant tree*
*Bright melody for me*
*Return.*

Here, Emily imagines that the flown bird – Sue – will return with 'Bright melody' for the poet. It appears at this stage as if the thought of her beloved's departure is only tolerable if she can persuade herself that the absence is in fact undertaken on her own behalf. This feels strained and narcissistic, as if without the solace of the making of the poem, the pain would become intolerable. At the age of twenty-three, it appears that Emily still feels like a baby bird, needing to be fed by other larger birds: ones with bright plumage, as in the 'panic attack' letter, or those returning with the gift of song, from lands to which Emily herself feels increasingly unable to travel. Yet alongside this vulnerability lies a curious strength, almost bloody-mindedness. She almost masochistically appears wedded to the 'darker spirit' that Jesus will not accept. She also threatens Sue with her superiority of spirit: she, not Susan, has the strength to continue alone, without Jesus and if necessary without Susan. When the poet says she has 'lived by this', she means perhaps that she has devoted her life to the truth of feeling, however intense, however idealised, and with whatever consequences. It is implied that Susan herself does not have the strength to live so courageously. Yet we should remember that Susan, without financial independence, was not in as privileged a position as Emily. And despite compromises Susan may have made, she continued to support and recognise Emily's gift. In an obituary about the poet her friend wrote, perhaps with a touch of envy as well as sympathy, that she turned as she got older 'to her own large wealth of individual resources for companionship, sitting thenceforth, as someone said of her, "in the light of her own fire."'

A fascinating short poem echoes something of the aggressive masochism Emily may have experienced from withdrawals made by those she loved too idealistically. Written in 1863, when her own habit of withdrawal was more advanced, it also says something about the exhilarating horror (to echo a phrase from one of her best-known poems) that she herself might have experienced in exerting control over those she saw or did not see.

*Rehearsal to Ourselves*
*Of a Withdrawn Delight –*
*Affords a Bliss like Murder –*
*Omnipotent – Acute –*

*We will not drop the Dirk –*
*Because We love the Wound*
*The Dirk Commemorate – Itself*
*Remind Us that We died –*

* * *

Emily wrote to Susan more buoyantly in 1855, from Washington. The poet had undertaken a rare trip to accompany her father and sister. Edward was standing as a representative of a conservative, independent political party, and for the first time as a player on the national stage. His career in this role was short-lived, but its impact significant.

As far as his daughter was concerned, it brought her into contact with the man many think was one of the most important characters in her life. After three weeks in Washington, their father took his daughters to stay with their second cousin Eliza Coleman in Philadelphia. They remained for a further two weeks. It appears that this trip was a timely break from Emily's concerns about her friendship with Susan. It may also have been frustration with that dynamic that caused her to idealise somebody new. On 18th March 1855 Emily writes an animated letter to her friend Elizabeth Holland, telling her of the things she has seen, 'the elegance, the grandeur;' and says, 'We have had many pleasant times, and seen much that is fair, and heard much that is wonderful –'

'Wonderful' utterances may have fallen from the lips of Reverend Charles Wadsworth, a gifted preacher, who in his younger years had written poetry. Depressive of temperament and brilliant of mind, he made a deep impression, to the extent that we know that Emily sought his personal advice on an anxious matter, to which he responded with earnest concern, and also in that he visited her at least twice, once in 1860 or 1861 and then again in 1880. His move from Arch Street Presbyterian Church in Philadelphia to distant San Francisco in 1862 appears to have added to Emily's sense of loneliness and crisis at that time. Wadsworth was married, to Jane Locke, in an apparently happy union. Jane had been deeply impressed by her husband's presence in church before they married, and together they went on to have three children: Edith, born in 1858, Charles Junior born two years later, and Willie, born 1868.

Despite this, it is thought that he might have become Emily's lover either in reality or in her imagination, although the truth remains unknown. This rumour was in part spread by Martha Dickinson Bianchi, Susan's daughter, when she wrote a memoir of her aunt, *Emily Dickinson Face to Face*, which was published by Houghton Mifflin in 1932. Her view was that there was no doubt that the cause of Emily's becoming a recluse and adopting the habit of wearing a white dress was that she was the victim of a doomed love affair with began during her visit to Philadelphia: a match which was impossible because the man in question was already married. While it is tempting to believe what appears to be an authoritative account of events, subsequent scholarship has revealed Martha's account to be highly unreliable.

What is known is that after his death, Emily corresponded with a friend of Wadsworth's, James Dickson Clark, who sent her a photograph of him and with whom she had a deeply tender exchange. After James Clark's death, she continued the connection by writing to his younger bother, Charles. We shall examine the connection between Emily and Wadsworth more closely when we come to the 'Master' letters.

* * *

Emily returned to Amherst in late March 1855. A letter written later in that year to Jane Humphrey reveals a continuing need for Emily to revivify 'romantic' attachments that the other party had probably outgrown. This also shows a continuing sense of acute nostalgia and underlying anxiety. She writes to Jane, with whom she shared a bed as a child, on 16th October 1855:

> *How I wish you were mine, as you once were, when I had you in the morning, and when the sun went down, and was sure I should never go to sleep without a moment from you. I try to prize it, Jennie, when the loved are here, try to love* more, *and* faster, *and* dearer, *but when all are gone, seems as had I tried* harder, *they would have stayed with me.*

Emily's notion that had she tried harder those she loved would have stayed in Amherst is at once so omnipotent and so misguided that it is worth expanding. We will remember from Emily's letter to Abiah that when Sophia Holland died in 1844, Emily gave way to a 'fixed melancholy' when she realised she could not bring her back from the dead. This failed omnipotence might have been one source of the episode of depression that seems to have ensued. Might it also have been that she projected onto others her own extreme fidelity to Amherst? If she, Emily, loved her family so much that she was never able to leave them, then it would only follow that if her friends loved *her* as much, they too would never leave. Emily apparently refused to see Emily Fowler Ford when she visited Amherst in later life, this being just one example of her upsetting cherished friends. It is odd, on the one hand, that she refused to see others when she herself had been so sensitive to others' withdrawals. Yet there may have been a direct relationship between these two facts: that she found loss so painful that she had to be the one in control of the comings and goings.

Another thought about her refusal to leave her father's ground as time went by is that this was an unconscious form of punishment to parents who wanted her dutiful and over-protected within the Dickinson mansion. We should remember that neither of the other siblings left this arena either, and that after their father's death a form of mayhem ensued when Austin took up with a married lover. The masochistic and sadistic 'Bliss like a Murder' of withdrawal may have been at play here. To put it differently, it may have been as if she were saying to her father and mother, 'You don't want me to go? I will show you to what degree I will stay – even if it kills me.'

* * *

Before Susan and Austin were married, another dramatic change of circumstance befell the Dickinson household.

Edward apparently never recovered from having to sell the Homestead, for when he could afford it, fifteen years after moving to West Street, he bought it back from the ageing General Mack. Yet Edward's family had settled in and come to enjoy their no-longer-new home, and when the moment came, none but Edward appears to have been pleased to be going back. A revealing comment made by Emily in a letter to Austin four years before the repurchase, dated 23rd September 1851, refers to the Homestead as 'the ancient Mansion', and goes on:

> *I am glad we dont come home as we used, to this old castle. I could fancy that skeleton cats ever caught spectre rats in dim old nooks and corners, and when I hear the query concerning the pilgrim fathers – and imperturbable Echo merely answers* where, *it becomes a satisfaction to know that they are there, sitting stark and stiff in Deacon Mack's mouldering arm chairs.*

This is significant, as it reveals that Emily does not view the Homestead, as one might have supposed, with nostalgia; instead she associates it with the spectres of the pilgrim fathers, her forebears, rather than with a lost idyll. 'A Prison gets to be a friend –' she wrote, as we've seen, in 1862, making manifest, as she often does, the paradoxical relationship between her incarceration within the ancestral mansion, and her sometimes masochistically pleasurable experience of it.

Almost immediately after the move in late 1855, ill effects seem to have settled in, as is revealed in a letter of January 1856 sent to Emily's loyal friend and comforter Elizabeth Holland:

> *... I have another story, and lay my laughter all away, so that I can sigh. Mother has been an invalid since we came* home, *and Vinnie and I "regulated", and Vinnie and I "got settled", and still we keep our father's house, and mother lies upon the lounge, or sits in her easy chair. I don't know what her sickness is, for I am but a simple child, and frightened at myself.*

This is the letter, cited earlier, in which she goes on to refer to the wish to be 'a toddling daisy, whom all these problems of the dust might not terrify', and which shows a forewarning of psychological disturbance when she makes the plea, 'should my own machinery get slightly out of gear, *please*, kind ladies and gentlemen, some one stop the wheel, –'

In the riveting, sad passage about her mother, Emily emphasises 'home', to reflect that in fact it no longer feels like home. Their mother, ill with an undiagnosed state of ennui and depression, may have found the weight of history, various family strains and losses, and Edward's will, too much. She remained unwell for several years. 'Daisy', employed here, is a word Emily uses at a key moment later, when she drafts one of her desperate letters to 'Master'.

In 1855–7 we have no poems, and remarkably few letters, with none at all in 1857, which is striking. Cody posits the theory, unfashionable but nonetheless interesting, that Emily's silence in 1857 denotes a severe breakdown, precipitated by the psychic implications for her of Austin and Sue's marriage in July 1856. He considers that she experienced full blown and ongoing psychotic symptoms, recorded in the great works of 1861–3. Tempting as it is to analyse retrospectively the curious case of Emily Dickinson, we should also note that other biographers have argued closely, with equal conviction, that Emily's condition was, for example, agoraphobia, as posited in Maryanne M. Garbowsky's book *The House Without the Door: A Study of Emily Dickinson and the Illness of Agoraphobia*, or most recently epilepsy, as Lyndall Gordon's *Lives Like Loaded Guns: Emily Dickinson and Her Family's Feuds* suggests.

What we do know about this period is that Emily and Vinnie worked extremely hard to keep the Homestead going, and that the years 1855 to 1858 were testing in the extreme, resulting in Emily's emergence as a committed poet. As Habegger summarises, among the trials befalling the Dickinsons were the obscure and enduring nature of Emily's mother's collapse, the financial collapse of Aunt Lavinia's husband and a further wave of religious revivals. We do know that when she wrote to Mrs Joseph (Mary Emerson) Haven, wife of a graduate of Amherst and professor in Chicago, in the summer of 1858, Emily said she would visit if she could:

> *... leave home, or mother. I do not go out at all, lest father will come and miss me, or miss some little act, which I might forget, should I run away – Mother is much as usual. I know not what to hope of her. Please remember Vinnie and I, for we are perplexed often –*
>
> *Affy –*
>
> *Emilie –*

## *Herself to her a music*
## The Making of a Great Poet, 1858–63

Sue and Austin married in Geneva, New York, so Emily was spared, or denied, the wedding. The couple returned to Amherst, to settle in to the Evergreens in the summer of 1856 – a house built on Dickinson land, a few hundred metres from the Homestead. Sue, regardless of other Dickinson family troubles, established her home as a centre for visiting literati and other eminent friends. Ambitious and highly sociable, Susan created what amounted to a salon. In the early days, Emily's literary influence may well have contributed to the sense of drive and purpose. Susan and Austin's marriage, it seems, remained unconsummated for some time. Indeed, there is evidence to suggest that Susan had agreed to the match so long as she not be harassed into having sexual relations. Fear of the consequences of childbirth has been cited as a contributing factor to her anxiety in this area, a modern reader, however, might imagine that it may also have been that her own sexuality was more ambivalent than Austin had realised. When Austin took a lover, many years later in 1882/83 (an intense, remarkably open affair with a much younger married woman, which lasted until his death), his lover, Mabel, reported that he had told her that his marriage to Susan had been a sham from the first. In time, dramatic rumours circulated, fuelled by Mabel, that Susan was an alcoholic like her father, prone to bouts of violent bad temper, controlling, fickle and socially ambitious to an alienating degree, and unrewarding as an intimate. Certainly, Susan ruffled feathers. We cannot know how much of this is true, yet it is certain that life at the Evergreens became increasingly miserable for Austin, and that the relationship between the Dickinson sisters and the other house became increasingly fraught with unhappy complexity.

This future deterioration notwithstanding, there is evidence that in the early days of the marriage Emily's presence was welcome – on occasions at least – at the Evergreens, and that she would avail herself of its society.

Catherine Scott Turner, a young widow, stayed at Sue and Austin's home between January and February 1859 and returned for two more extended periods in 1861 and 1863. Her recollections, dating from many years later, give us a splendid picture of Emily in a surprisingly cheerful habitat, reminding us of the excitable and vivacious Emily of her schooldays:

> Those celestial evenings in the Library – the blazing *wood* fire – *Emily* – *Austin*, – the music – the rampant fun – the inextinguishable laughter, the uproarious spirits of our chosen – our most congenial circle... Emily with her dog, & Lantern! often at the piano playing weird & beautiful melodies, all from her own inspiration, oh! she was a choice spirit.

On one occasion Catherine, known as Kate, recalled that the partying went on so late that Edward appeared to take his almost thirty-year-old daughter home. It seems astonishing to us that a grown up need escorting a few hundred yards. Yet this image of her father, presumably sitting up in his wing of the Homestead, looking out for her return rather than delighting in her playful sociability, tells us much about his continued controlling influence over his remarkable child.

Another important friend to have entered Emily's life through the Evergreens was Samuel Bowles, the influential owner and editor-in-chief of *The Springfield Republican*. Flirtatious and in an unsatisfying marriage, Bowles loved powerful women. At one point he was a candidate for the male figure in the Master letters, although this theory is now generally considered to be out of date. An important literary correspondent for many years, Bowles received many poems from Emily until his death in 1878, after which Emily took up corresponding with his son.

Yet on other important occasions, Emily was not present. The eminent Emerson himself made a visit in 1857, and Emily did not attend. One view is that she was too mentally ill or withdrawn to make it, but it may also have been that Susan's unpredictability was at play. On some occasions it may have suited her to invite her curiously bewitching sister-in-law, and on others it may have felt better to leave her out of it. Sewall records a view, expressed by Alfred E. Stearns, a resident of Amherst and a young man when Emily was in her late forties, that 'snob' Susan was 'ashamed' of her eccentric, spinster sisters-in-law. Yet it may also have been, especially when they were young, that Susan wanted to be Queen Bee, and that Emily, whom many considered a 'choice spirit', and who had a habit of managing to spark up correspondences with some of Susan's most illustrious guests, may have posed competition that was not always wanted. Certainly, until the end, Emily sent notes to her sister-in-law reinstating her, for example, as 'Only Woman in the World' (1875).

In the summer of 1858, against the background of Sue and Austin building their apparently mutually powerful dominion, Emily also began to build. In the words of R.W. Franklin, who edited the most authoritatively complete *The Poems of Emily Dickinson* in 1998 (The Belknap Press of Harvard University Press), she now began her first 'major stocktaking… a sifting and winnowing of her entire corpus'. She reviewed all her work and made clean copies of selected poems on good stationery. She sewed together the pages of four sheets, with several poems on one sheet, and thus began the practice that she kept up through to 1865. The booklets made during this period, commonly known as fascicles, contained almost eight hundred poems. Intermittent exposure to the new circle in Sue's household may have served as a spur to a private ambition. Increased output, and the development of an increasingly original poetic voice, must also have inspired her. It is noteworthy that Sue herself continued to be the muse behind a number of the poems. In 1858, Emily writes a poem in which she names her sister-in-law:

*One Sister have I in the house –*
*And one a hedge away.*
*There's only one recorded –*
*But both belong to me.*

*One came the road that I came –*
*And wore my last year's gown –*
*The other, as a bird her nest*
*Builded our hearts among.*

*She did not sing as we did –*
*It was a different tune –*
*Herself to her a music*
*As Bumble bee of June.*

*Today is far from childhood,*
*But up and down the hills,*
*I held her hand the tighter –*
*Which shortened all the miles –*

*And still her hum*
*The years among,*
*Deceives the Butterfly;*
*And in her Eye*
*The Violets lie,*
*Mouldered this many May -*
*I spilt the dew,*

*But took the morn –*
*I chose this single star*
*From out the wide night's numbers –*
*Sue – forevermore!*

'Sue – forevermore!' Emily's devotion still runs high, despite the growing realisation that 'She did not sing as we did – / It was a different tune –'.

Emily's poetry was increasingly becoming a place where she could deposit, work through and make something remarkable of her extreme emotions, and her heightened observations about the natural world, as well as her unconventional inner world.

Next to this, a small poem of the same year, 'Adrift! A little boat adrift!', asks 'Will *no* one guide a little boat / Unto the nearest town?', imagining two endings for two different boats: the first:

*... gave up it's strife*
*And gurgled down and down.*

while the second:

*... o'erspent with gales –*
*Retrimmed it's masts – redecked it's sails –*
*And shot – exultant on!*

The course of Emily's own inner life was still volatile, as she found it difficult to tell if she were gurgling 'down and down' or 'exultant'. These vicissitudes were not going to become any easier to manage.

The rest of the poems produced in 1858–60 contain expressions of alarm at her narrowing life, in poems such as 'I cautious, scanned my little life – / I winnowed what would fade'; of acute pain, as in 'A *wounded* Deer – leaps highest – / I've heard the Hunter tell –'; of exuberant hope about her life, as in ''Tis so much joy! 'Tis so much joy!'; of fear about failure, as in 'Success is counted sweetest/By those who ne'er succeed'; and of mysterious expressions intimating spiritual journeying, along with many other themes, including the introduction of the theme of a male lover, which we will examine later. Yet it seems as if Susan is the main emotional muse. Note, for example, the tantalisingly coy creation of 1859, which seems again to speak of a secret passion for a woman, in which a robbing and a betrayal have occurred:

*So bashful when I spied her!*
*So pretty – so ashamed!*
*So hidden in her leaflets*
*Lest anybody find –*

*So breathless till I passed her –*
*So helpless when I turned*
*And bore her struggling, blushing,*
*Her simple haunts beyond!*

*For whom I robbed the Dingle –*
*For whom betrayed the Dell –*
*Many, will doubtless ask me –*
*But I shall never tell!*

Alongside poetic activity from this time, it is important to note that the first of three letters, written to an anonymous 'Master', is dated to the spring or the summer of 1858, or thereabouts. These letters, in contrast to some of the poems, seem to concern a heterosexual relationship, real or imagined. The intended recipient remains uncertain and some argue that the addressee in the Master letters (a second from circa 1861 and the third circa early 1862) never existed. To add to the mystery, it is not known whether these letters were ever sent. We will explore them more fully shortly.

# *And every One unbared a Nerve*
# Breakdown and the great poems

Susan and Austin had their first child, Ned, five years after marriage, in 1861. Susan may have been pregnant before this, if reports spread by Mabel Loomis Todd, Austin's lover, are to be believed. Alarmingly, amongst Todd's claims was that one of the sources of Austin's extreme unhappiness came from the fact that his wife had actively aborted four previous conceptions. Indeed, Todd claimed that Susan had tried to abort Ned, and that the failure of this attempt was to be blamed for the child's epilepsy. Whatever the truth of this (and Gordon vehemently argues that Todd is not to be trusted) its importance lies in giving a sense of the confusing misery that later enveloped Susan and Austin's life, and in turn affected the poet's. Inspired by the occasion of Ned's birth on 19th June 1861, Emily sent an extraordinary poem to Susan:

> *Is it true, dear Sue?*
> *Are there* two?
> *I should'nt like to come*
> *For fear of joggling Him!*
> *If you could shut him up*
> *In a Coffee Cup,*
> *Or tie him to a pin*
> *Till I got in –*
> *Or make him fast*

*To "Toby's" fist –*
*Hist! Whist! I'd come!*

Strikingly, over and over again in her work and communication, Emily goes for the jugular, the psychic truth of what she feels, as opposed to anything polite expected of her. She has a horror of false feeling – the 'dimity' convictions of the gentlewomen in a famous poem of hers about religion – and she holds nothing back. If we are to believe Susan's daughter, Emily's bluntness could upset even her brother, but Sue was less easy to rattle. Martha, Susan and Austin's daughter, observes in her memoir tha her father 'shrank' from some of the tasteless stories her aunt told.

There is no sign that Susan took against Emily for this note, and indeed its openness assumes intimacy. A few months afterwards she and Emily had an exchange about one of Emily's most famous poems. Perhaps there was something in Emily's extremity that Sue admired, that she recognised in a different form in herself. The poem Emily sent was about death, perhaps an odd choice of subject to send to a new mother. It was as if Emily was asking not to be forgotten now that the baby had arrived, and asking Susan not to forget a primary commitment to literature, which she hoped they both might continue to share. It ran:

*Safe in their Alabaster Chambers,*
*Untouched by Morning*
*And untouched by noon,*
*Sleep the meek members of the Resurrection,*
*Rafter of satin*
*And Roof of stone.*

*Light laughs the breeze*
*In her Castle above them,*
*Babbles the Bee in a stolid Ear,*

*Pipe the Sweet Birds in ignorant cadence, –*
*Ah, what sagacity perished here!*

Sue must have responded saying that she found the second verse problematic, for Emily wrote back saying, 'Perhaps this verse would please you better – Sue – / Emily –' The rewrite read:

*Safe in their Alabaster Chambers,*
*Untouched by Morning –*
*And untouched by Noon –*
*Lie the meek members of the Resurrection –*
*Rafter of satin – and Roof of Stone –*

*Grand go the Years – in the Crescent – about them –*
*Worlds scoop their Arcs –*
*And Firmaments – row –*
*Diadems – drop – and Doges – surrender –*
*Soundless as dots – on a Disc of Snow –*

Sue responded immediately to this new version, writing:

*I am not suited dear Emily with the second verse – It is remarkable as the chain lightening that blinds us hot nights in the Southern sky but it does not go with the ghostly shimmer of the first verse as well as the other one – It just occurs to me that the first verse is complete in itself it needs no other, and can't be coupled – Strange things always go alone – as there is only one Gabriel and one Sun – You never made a peer for that verse, and* I guess *you[r] kingdom does'nt hold one – I always go to the fire and get warm after thinking of it, but I never* can *again – The flowers are sweet and bright and look as if they would kiss one – ah, they expect a humming-bird – Thanks for them of course – and not thanks only recognition either – Did it ever occur to you that is all there is here after all – "Lord that I may receive my sight" –*

*Susan is tired making* bibs *for her bird – her ring-dove – he will paint my cheeks when I am old to pay me –*
*Sue –*
*Pony Express*

Sue's response is particularly intriguing as we have so little left of her side of any correspondence. It gives us a rare insight into their connection. First, it is noteworthy that Sue's own writing style seems in ways to mirror Emily's, with erratic punctuation driven more by feeling and thought-process than technical accuracy. Also, the flight of fancy about the humming bird reveals a romantic and poetic sense in her own nature. We get a glimpse of what Emily loved in Susan. The humming bird offering a kiss in Sue's note is an extraordinarily sexual image, and it may be that she had in mind as she wrote it the kisses that Emily used to long to bestow upon her. Also important here is the reference to being tired making bibs: while motherhood was, despite her worst fears perhaps, a source of pleasure in her 'ring-dove', it was also a source of tedium. It is often assumed that it was Emily who envied Sue – her marriage, her children, her social capacity – but we should not forget that Sue may well have envied Emily's single-minded commitment to a more monastic life: a life dedicated to her craft. Susan comments that 'Strange things always go alone – as there is only one Gabriel and one Sun –', and makes the astute critical observation that the first verse 'needs no other'. Perhaps she admired, as she indicated in her obituary of Emily, her strength in remaining alone, however difficult that choice had been.

It may also have been envy that caused Susan to quip, in relation to a suitable second verse, 'I *guess* you[r] kingdom does'nt hold one –'. Yet Emily does have a kingdom, which Susan recognises. In response to her sister-in-law's critique Emily sends a third attempt at a second verse, demonstrating the life-blood reciprocity of their literary relationship:

*Is* this frostier?

*Springs – shake the sills –*
*But – the Echoes – stiffen –*
*Hoar – is the Window –*
*And numb – the Door –*
*Tribes of Eclipse – in Tents of Marble*
*Staples of Ages – have buckled – there –*

*Dear Sue –*
*Your praise is good – to me – because I* know *it* knows *and* suppose – *it* means –
*Could I make you and Austin – proud – sometime – a great way off – 'twould give me taller feet –*
*Here is a crumb – for the "Ring dove" – and a spray for* his Nest, *a little while ago* – just – "Sue."

Emily expresses here a rare direct desire to 'make you and Austin – proud' through her writing.

However, Susan had problems of her own. Ned proved to be epileptic, and an extremely difficult child to manage. Her relations with Austin were deteriorating, and Emily, with her neediness and heightened, nervous sensibilities, would begin to be a problematic guest. It seems that at this point their relationship shifted. Perhaps there was an incident when Emily did go to visit, and was not allowed in, for shortly after the above exchange about 'Safe in their Alabaster Chambers', Emily wrote a note to Susan:

*Could* I *– then – shut the door –*
*Lest* my *beseeching face – at last –*
*Rejected – be – of* Her?

A poem of the following year, 1862, might reveal how painful exchanges with Susan had become:

*She dealt her pretty words like Blades –*
*How glittering they shone –*
*And every One unbared a Nerve*
*Or wantoned with a Bone –*

In a letter of 25th April 1862, Emily famously refers to a 'terror – since September' of the previous year. Whatever the source of her anguish, and the timing of it, in 1861 the rate at which her poems were produced increased, rising even more in 1862 (227 poems), 1863 (295), 1864 (98) and 1865 (229). The intensification was both in output and in content, the poems revealing states of extreme anguish, rapture, hysteria and possibly delusion. Emily herself had felt in her early twenties, and continued to feel, like a child. As Sue kept herself to herself, and stopped inviting Emily over with such regularity, Emily felt increasingly shut out, ironically and traumatically from the house that was only 'a hedge away', as she describes it in 'One sister have I in the house'. It was in part Emily's fear of being rejected that caused her to withdraw – and this practice of withdrawing and hiding, even from those she loved, became increasingly entrenched.

# 'tonight, Master'
# Master Letters

1861, the year of Ned's birth, was also the year of the second Master letter. In the edited *Letters* it appears just after the 'Is it true, dear Sue?' poem, written on the occasion of Ned's birth.

While there is an argument that the centralisation of the Master drafts in Emily's biography might be falsely distorting, it would not be responsible for any biographer to omit them or minimise their significance at least to scholars. They were found in her papers, placed among her poems after her death, and it may well be that they were experiments in fiction, as opposed to expressions of authentic emotion pertaining to any one recipient. With this warning, readers should decide for themselves what to make of the mysterious missives – apparently heterosexual, though it has been argued otherwise – and their extreme attitudinising, as a fragile female in relation to a potent, beloved man. It may have been that fear of a second wave of loss of Sue as denoted by the birth of Ned forced a heterosexual identity to the surface as if in reaction formation, as Freud would have termed it, to the crisis of sexual identity faced. Alternatively, fear of losing out in the area of intimate love could have encouraged Emily to make what emotional drama she could out of feelings for an unidentifiable male, or composite male fantasy. Or, of course, she could have been conducting a clandestine affair.

The first Master letter, dated to 1858, is relatively calm in tone, and appears to have been written to somebody in her orbit who has made contact after a period of silence: 'Dear Master/ I am ill, but grieving more that you are ill… I thought perhaps you were in Heaven, and when you spoke again, it seemed quite sweet, and wonderful, and surprised me…' Emily, or the 'I' in the letter draft, appears previously to have sent this person flowers, for she says, 'You ask me what my flowers said – then they were disobedient – I gave them messages.'

The second letter, written shortly after the birth of Ned, is again addressed to the unidentified 'Master'. Obscure and puzzling, it seems to be etched out of pain:

> *Master.*
>
> *If you saw a bullet hit a Bird – and he told you he was'nt shot – you might weep at his courtesy, but you would certainly doubt his word.*
>
> *One drop more from the gash that stains your Daisy's bosom – then would you believe?*

This letter is more chopped up syntactically than many in her correspondence (and most are grammatically eccentric enough). Descriptions of what appear to be real events merge with sentences that veer on the incomprehensible.

Yet certain passages seem clear enough in their meaning. Here she speaks in earnest of a love, and a regret that she cannot adopt the 'Queen's place', the place of wife, in Master's life.

> *I am older – tonight, Master – but the love is the same – so are the moon and the crescent. If it had been God's will that I might breathe where you breathed – and find the place – myself – at night – if I (can) never forget that I am not with you – and that sorrow and frost are nearer than I – if I wish with a might I cannot repress – that mine were the Queen's place… the prank of the Heart at play on the Heart – in holy Holiday – is forbidden me –*

She goes on to say that she will wait as long as necessary 'till my hazel hair is dappled – and you carry the cane –' for him, adding, 'What would you do with me if I came "in white?" Have you the little chest to put the Alive – in?'

The third Master letter, dated to early 1862, is even more bizarre. It refers to a parting, suggesting that whoever Master was, he had visited. She fears, as she often did in relation to those she loved, that she has caused offence. Referring to herself again as 'Daisy', she reminds us of the wish expressed in her letter to Mrs Holland, that she could be 'a toddling daisy, whom all these problems of the dust might not terrify':

> *Oh, did I offend it – [Did'nt it want me to tell it the truth] Daisy – Daisy – offend it – who bends her smaller life to his (it's) meeker (lower) every day – who only asks – a task – [who] something to do for love of it – some little way she cannot guess to make that master glad –*
>
> *A love so big it scares her, rushing among her small heart – pushing aside the blood and leaving her faint (all) and white in the gust's arm –*
>
> *Daisy – who never flinched thro' that awful parting, but held her life so tight he should not see the wound – who would have sheltered him in her childish bosom (Heart) – only it was'nt big eno' for a Guest so large...*
>
> *I've got a cough as big as a thimble – but I dont care for that – I've got a Tomahawk in my side but that dont hurt me much. [If you] Her master stabs her more –*

Here she is experiencing 'A love so big it scares her', and says that her 'childish bosom... was'nt big eno' for a Guest so large.'

Who this lover was, or indeed whether he was real, is not known, nor is it known whether or not the Master letters were ever sent. However, if one is to opt for a single candidate, the Reverend Charles Wadsworth, whom Emily saw preach in Philadelphia in 1855, is the one who has received the most backing.

We know that Wadsworth visited Emily some time in 1860 or 1861, which might make sense of 'an awful parting'. We also know that he sent her a brief note, placed in Johnson's edition of the *Letters* immediately following her third Master letter of 1862. In addition, towards the end of his life he visited Emily unannounced in 1882, as if to make peace with her before their deaths. He was also a man with the kind of gravitas that would have inspired admiration in Emily, and had he, although married, shown any sign of particular interest in her, such an interest might have acted like a spark upon a fire set ready to burn.

His note to her, dated to 1862 reads:

*My Dear Miss Dickenson*

*I am distressed beyond measure at your note, received this moment, – I can only imagine the affliction which has befallen, or is now befalling you.*

*Believe me, be what it may, you have all my sympathy, and my constant, earnest prayers.*

*I am very, very anxious to learn more definitely of your trial – and though I have no right to intrude upon your sorrow yet I beg you to write me, though it be but a word.*

*In great haste*
*Sincerely and most*
*Affectionately* Yours –

Did Emily misread the emphasised 'Yours' and make more of it than was meant? Did they write in formal code to hide expressed feelings? Or is the letter as it appears, in fact from a bemused but kindly onlooker? As Lavinia burned virtually all the letters Emily received, at her sister's instruction, and as no letters from Emily have been released from the Wadsworth family, the secret, if there is one, went with them both to the grave.

* * *

As if to augment the impression of the existence of a real Master in her life, a number of poems erupt into being that seem to talk of a meeting, a passionate internal wedding, and a renunciation between two lovers. These are etched into her canon, and puzzle her readers.

One of the most blatant of these poems about a secret marriage Emily sent to her great friend the editor Samuel Bowles in early 1862. This was perhaps to seek attention for her extreme internal state. At the end of the poem, she urges him to keep her confidence and writes:

*Here's – what I had to "tell you" –*
*You will tell no other? Honor – is it's*
*own pawn –*

This communication feels surprisingly playful if it truly denotes the confiding of so great a secret. It is also a confusing communication, marrying both an exultant feeling at the 'Title divine', and profound ambivalence (or worse) in the second half, when it refers to being 'Born – Bridalled – Shrouded –/ In a Day –. Is this really about her own internal marriage? Or is she simply confiding to Bowles her views about what being a wife would mean? Surely she is not in favour of women 'Stroking the Melody' and asking their husbands, 'Is this – the way?'

The poem, as it was sent and recorded by Johnson in his edition of the letters, reads:

*Title divine – is mine!*
*The Wife – without the Sign!*
*Acute Degree – conferred on me –*
*Empress of Calvary!*
*Royal – all but the Crown!*
*Betrothed – without the swoon*
*God sends us Women –*
*When you – hold – Garnet to Garnet –*

*Gold – to Gold –*
*Born – Bridalled – Shrouded –*
*In a Day –*
*"My Husband" – women say –*
*Stroking the Melody –*
*Is* this – *the way?*

A variant of this poem was sent to Susan, about the same time. The timing of these striking poetic concoctions, proliferating chronologically we think alongside the Master letters, is not insignificant. For other examples of poems about a symbolic marriage, see 'Tie the strings to my Life, My Lord,', 'Of all the Souls that stand create –/I have Elected – One – ', 'Ourselves were wed one summer – dear –', 'Mine – by the Right of the White Election!' and 'He touched me, so I live to know'. It may of course be that Wadsworth's visit in 1860/1, did mark a real love affair, but about this we cannot be sure. What we do know is that in her immediate, everyday world, Emily had been disturbed by the birth of Ned, and that Susan was increasingly preoccupied.

Emily may well have felt a natural panic about what the future, once dreamed about with such excitement, really held in store for her. Emily's inability to grasp Sue's increasing distance emerges time and time again in the poems alongside some of those to a man, which we have just explored. It is as if Emily is struggling to maintain the love she once felt with such passionate intensity for her sister-in-law, which she feels cannot simply have disappeared. Whereas the poems and Master letters written to a male lover feel unreal in any detail pertaining to the loved object, by contrast, those poems and continuing letters and scraps to Sue feel utterly real, full of pathos, love, disappointment and, touchingly, an enduring commitment despite everything. Yet any meaningful hope of a sustaining triangle with her brother and sister-in-law, with Emily herself potently central to their happiness, was by now not possible. The result of this realisation appears to have resulted in a rapid and painful shrinkage of her already contracted world: a world she found it increasingly difficult to escape, except through writing. A world that was both 'prison' and 'friend.'

The Master letters and identity of the male lover will remain a mystery, yet there is no doubt, as was posited in the Overview, that a real symbolic 'marriage' was made with her poetry, her 'loved Philology!' Those she loved were in literary terms metaphorical spouses, and we as readers, congregation to that central commitment. As is the case with many writers, Emily found her muses where she could, and grafted onto them the high emotion they inspired, in the form of dazzling words that have been handed down to us through time.

# *After great pain, a formal feeling comes* – The Martyr Poets and the 'Terrible' poems

The pain of her world closing in on her helped to create the poetry that made Emily great. It is a cruel paradox, but one that Emily understood when she wrote 'The Martyr Poets – did not tell –/ But wrought their Pang in syllable –'. It has become unfashionable to talk about Emily's suffering, as if this constitutes a denial of the element of choice she exerted over how she lived her life, and yet to deny the degree of difficulty is to fail to acknowledge the extent of her achievement. It is arguable that most writers have an ambivalent relationship to the peculiar demands that being a writer makes, as has been expressed by many in that profession. Samuel Johnson, for example, said that 'No man but a blockhead ever wrote, except for money', implying that writing was not something to pursue for the fun of it, and Margaret Atwood, replying to an interview question for *January Magazine* in 2000 about what it was like to be a writer, said that it was 'dark in there.' Artists often also express the view that they do not select their profession, but that their profession selects them. For women in particular the split between domestic activity and creativity can create tension, as was famously argued by Virginia Woolf when she posited in her essay *A Room of One's Own* that women, like men, need their own 'space' in which to create. In Emily Dickinson's case, her talent and quiet determination to 'live by this' – the gift given to her 'by the gods' and her uncompromising authenticity of spirit – had driven her into a complicated, isolated corner that would, as perhaps she knew, engender her greatest work.

Sylvia Plath, that other great American poet, who ultimately, unlike Emily, failed to survive her mental anguish and committed suicide, recognised a link some artists experience between pain and greatness. She wrote in her journals on 11th May 1958, 'Oh, only left to myself, what a poet I will flay myself in to.' Whether she had meant to take this risk or not, Emily's 'love' of 'the danger' had landed her in a precarious psychic situation.

In various poems she explores the relationship between her increasing loneliness and her curious, almost religious pleasure in it. In the sublimely paradoxical work that expresses this most clearly, she writes in 1862:

*It might be lonelier*
*Without the Loneliness –*
*I'm so accustomed to my Fate –*
*Perhaps the Other – Peace –*

*Would interrupt the Dark –*
*And crowd the little Room –*
*Too scant – by Cubits – to contain*
*The Sacrament – of Him*

*I am not used to Hope –*
*It might intrude opon –*
*It's sweet parade – blaspheme the place –*
*Ordained to Suffering –*

*It might be easier*
*To fail – with Land in Sight –*
*Than gain – my Blue Peninsula –*
*To perish – of Delight –*

The gravity and quality of the writing is improving, her vocation underway. Another poem says:

*I cannot live with You –*
*It would be Life –*
*And Life is over there –*
*Behind the Shelf*

This unique work ends with a dark, metaphysical twist, poignant to a sublime degree:

*So we must meet apart –*
*You there – I – here –*
*With just the Door ajar*
*That Oceans are – and Prayer –*
*And that White Sustenance –*
*Despair –*

This work is made more moving knowing as we do that Emily did sometimes engage with people, through an 'ajar' door. Creating such alchemical masterpieces as these would certainly also have provided Emily with 'White Sustenance'. It is the sustenance gambled on when she 'ventured all opon a throw!'

Yet there were certainly times of almost unendurable darkness, and mental singularity, which are also recorded in the work. Emily's poetry had been startlingly original before 1861–2, and as we have seen she had started to collect her work in earnest from 1858, but the work of the years 1861–5, in particular 1861–3, sees not only an enormously increased rate of production, but also some of her greatest writing, upon the strength of which her reputation could stand alone. It may be, as some surmise, that the rapid rate of this production was a symptom of the kind of hyperactivity often seen in the aftermath of a serious breakdown. Much of the work was written at a tremendous rate on scraps of paper ranging from the backs of bills to chocolate wrappers, anything she could lay her hands on. Or perhaps her gift had simply gestated, and was ready to come out fully formed.

Before we look at some of the 'terrible' poems – to borrow from a term used to describe the 'terrible sonnets' that Gerard Manley Hopkins wrote to record a crisis of great magnitude, sonnets upon which his reputation could have rested – we should consider that the comparable period in Emily's life coincided with the Civil War. Violent hostility divided America between 1861 and 1865, a brilliant poetic account of which can be found in the remarkable epic poem *John Brown's Body: An Invocation* by John Vincent Benét, published in 1928. Whilst it is often said that Emily Dickinson was not interested in external events, more recently critics have considered her position again. A study such as that by Peggy Henderson Murphy, with a title that reveals much: 'Isolated But Not Oblivious: A Re-evaluation of Emily Dickinson's Relationship to the Civil War' will posit more complex views.

There are a few poems that speak directly of War, such as 'It feels a shame to be Alive –/When Men so brave – are dead –', but most concerned with battle use it as a metaphor for her personal state. One poem of particular interest, is 'Me from Myself – to banish –'. This is interpreted by both Cody and Garbowsky as evidence of violent internal disturbance, a splitting of self from self that denotes to the former biographer psychosis, and to the latter, agoraphobic dissolution. Either of them may be right, but it is important to remember that America too was assaulting itself, and that the solution of peace must have seemed impossible at times.

*Me from Myself – to banish –*
*Had I Art –*
*Invincible My Fortress*
*Unto All Heart –*

*But since Myself – assault Me –*
*How have I peace*
*Except by subjugating*
*Consciousness?*

*And since We're Mutual Monarch*
*How this be*
*Except by Abdication –*
*Me – of Me –?*

The Romantic aesthetic, spread by Emerson in America, contained philosophies concerning the poet's unconscious, osmotic relationship with nature, but also with the human sphere, and currents of philosophical and political thought. A poem such as Coleridge's 'Eolian Harp' expresses this:

*And what if all of animated nature*
*Be but organic Harps diversely fram'd,*
*That tremble into thought, as o'er them sweeps*
*Plastic and vast, one intellectual breeze,*
*At once the Soul of each, and God of all?*

There is a strong argument to be made that although Emily did not often address the subject of the Civil War directly, in either poems or letters – and when she did she did so sometimes facetiously – the tensions of the age were nonetheless present in her personal extremities. These were expressed in a period of extreme difficulty, which coincided with the beginning of the fighting.

At the age of thirty-two, also during this period, Emily wrote the lightning poem cited in the first chapter of this book, and worth revisiting, now, and reconsidering in the light of what we know about Emily as she was writing it. One of many 'terrible' poems, this nonetheless acts as an example of a kind of dateless pain, the relentless persecutory nature of that which her mind had suffered, or still suffered.

*It struck me – every Day –*
*The Lightning was as new*
*As if the Cloud that instant slit*
*And let the Fire through –*

*It burned Me – in the Night –*
*It Blistered to My Dream –*
*It sickened fresh opon my sight –*
*With every Morn that came –*

*I thought that Storm – was brief –*
*The Maddest – quickest by –*
*But Nature lost the Date of This –*
*And left it in the Sky –*

Now, we can measure this against other mature works, which speak of a similar, a-chronological condition:

*Pain – has an Element of Blank –*
*It cannot recollect*
*When it begun – Or if there were*
*A time when it was not –*

*It has no Future – but itself –*
*It's Infinite contain*
*It's Past – enlightenment to perceive*
*New Periods – Of Pain.*

Another great 'terrible' poem is uncertain when pain began, or when it will end, and refers to 'mechanical feet' that go round. It appears as if the catastrophe Emily feared in the letter of early 1856 to Mrs Elizabeth Holland, which asks for 'ladies and gentlemen' to protect her from her machinery getting out of control, has occurred:

*After great pain, a formal feeling comes –*
*The Nerves sit ceremonious, like Tombs –*
*The stiff Heart questions 'was it He, that bore,'*
*And 'Yesterday, or Centuries before'?*

*The Feet, mechanical, go round –*
*A Wooden way*
*Or Ground, or Air, or Ought,*
*Regardless grown –*
*A Quartz contentment, like a stone –*

*This is the Hour of Lead –*
*Remembered, if outlived,*
*As Freezing persons, recollect the Snow –*
*First – Chill – then Stupor – then the letting go –*

We also see that this mindless, mechanical self experiences a stony contentment. We are reminded of Emily's experience of Sue as stone-hearted, and of the stoniness she felt when threatened by abandonment. Cody and Garbowsky painstakingly and cogently analyse at length a large number of the poems concerning extreme mental states. Gordon argues the case for epilepsy. Whatever the medical diagnosis of her pain – if a single diagnosis be possible, itself doubtful – we must note that the poems, brave, alarming, articulate, original and astonishing, are what cause modern readers to admire her. We now know more than was known in the mid nineteenth century about the myriad ways in which the mind can become distorted, unbalanced and depressed – with each condition being ultimately unique to the sufferer. Emily endured whatever befell her without the benefit of psychoanalytic tools and advanced psychiatry, and her private courage resulted in her 'golden dream' – the alchemical transposition of unfathomable difficulty into nuggets of great poetry.

'The Brain – is wider than the Sky –' wrote Emily, beginning a poem cited in full in chapter two. She had hope that the strength of her mind would be enough to contain opposites, idealisations, and to create a habitat in which she could abide omnipotent. Coleridge, in his poem 'Dejection: An Ode', expresses upset at the failure of his 'shaping spirit of Imagination' to abide, when he is assaulted by distress. One could argue that it was the endeavour of the Romantics to try to sustain themselves with the superior strength of their inner worlds over the outer, and that the failure of this ideal of omnipotence was a source of pain. To quote Coleridge more fully:

*There was a time when, though my path was rough,*
*This joy within me dallied with distress,*
*And all misfortunes were but as the stuff*
*Whence Fancy made me dreams of happiness:*
*For hope grew round me, like the twining vine,*
*And fruits, and foliage, not my own, seemed mine.*
*But now afflictions bow me down to earth:*
*Nor care I that they rob me of my mirth,*
*But oh! each visitation*
*Suspends what Nature gave me at my birth,*
*My shaping spirit of Imagination.*
*For not to think of what I needs must feel,*
*But to be still and patient, all I can;*
*And haply by abstruse research to steal*
*From my own nature all the natural man –*
*This was my sole resource, my only plan:*
*Till that which suits a part infects the whole,*
*And now is almost grown the habit of my soul.*

Like Coleridge, Emily had had an 'only plan', 'to live by this' – the high authenticity of her feelings and dedication to her Muse, and when high, adolescent idealisation of Susan gave way; when the 'Master', real or otherwise, did not provide any kind of satisfaction in the world, and as war ravaged the country just beyond the bounds of home, Emily's mind also felt as if it were giving way. In addition, she increasingly found that she could not control the anxiety provoked when trying to manage normal, social interaction. Emily's brain may have led her to places she preferred not to visit, but nonetheless, like a hunter, she continued to track its activity wherever it took her. The precision with which she did this causes a modern reader to imagine that she might have made an excellent psychoanalyst had she been born later. The courage is tangible. The pains of hell were upon her, and these, like Whitman, she translated 'into a new tongue'.

Let us finish this section by witnessing without further comment, a few of the places that her mind took her to.

*I felt a Cleaving in my Mind –*
*As if my Brain had split –*
*I tried to match it – Seam by Seam –*
*But could not make them fit -*

*The thought behind, I strove to join*
*Unto the thought before –*
*But Sequence ravelled out of Sound -*
*Like Balls – opon a Floor –*

*

*The first Day's Night had come –*
*And grateful that a thing*
*So terrible – had been endured –*
*I told my Soul to sing –*

*She said her strings were snapt –*
*Her Bow – to atoms blown –*
*And so to mend her – gave me work*
*Until another Morn –*

*And then – a Day as huge*
*As Yesterdays in pairs,*
*Unrolled it's horror in my face –*
*Until it blocked my eyes –*

*My Brain – begun to laugh –*
*I mumbled – like a fool –*
*And tho' 'tis Years ago – that Day –*
*My Brain keeps giggling – still.*

*And Something's odd – within –*
*That person that I was –*
*And this One – do not feel the same –*
*Could it be Madness – this?*

*

*I felt a Funeral, in my Brain,*
*And Mourners to and fro*
*Kept treading – treading – till it seemed*
*That Sense was breaking through –*

*And when they all were seated,*
*A Service, like a Drum –*
*Kept beating – beating – till I thought*
*My mind was going numb –*

*And then I heard them lift a Box*
*And creak across my Soul*
*With those same Boots of Lead, again,*
*Then Space – began to toll,*

*As all the Heavens were a Bell,*
*And Being, but an Ear,*
*And I, and Silence, some strange Race*
*Wrecked, solitary, here –*

*And then a Plank in Reason, broke,*
*And I dropped down, and down –*
*And hit a World, at every plunge,*
*And Finished knowing – then –*

## *Are you too deeply occupied to say if my Verse is alive?* The search of a great writer for a worthy critic and mentor

One of the things that Emily 'Finished knowing – then –', to quote again from 'I felt a funeral, in my Brain', may have been that she had indeed, by now, produced poetry that was potentially of serious literary worth. It is important to note that while much is rightly made of her state of mind during 1857–63, particularly 1861–2, she had produced poems not only about feeling mad, but also about heightened passion, both love for and disenchantment with Susan, eternity, nature and other surprising subjects, such as spiders. She continued to be capable of sustaining a number of contradictory states simultaneously. Whatever the sources of her inspiration, by April 1862 she had a body of work containing more than 300 poems. Starvation of a satisfactory critic in Sue as their relations became less reliable may have spurred her to seek advice from more objective and professional quarters.

Emily first wrote to Higginson on 15th April 1862. Her correspondence with this prolific American writer and liberal campaigner, is one of the most valuable in the history of American literature. Higginson, like Emerson, was a retired minister, and he engaged in the war effort as a soldier and a colonel. Emily came across Higginson when she read his 'Letter to a Young Contributor', the lead article in *The Atlantic Monthly* for April 1862, which offered practical advice to would-be new writers. Emily enclosed with her first letter four poems, 'Safe in their

Alabaster Chambers', 'The nearest Dream – recedes – unrealized –', 'We Play at Paste –' and 'I'll tell you how the Sun rose'. The letter is so beguiling and curious that it is worth citing in full:

*15 April 1862*

*Mr Higginson,*

*Are you too deeply occupied to say if my Verse is alive?*

*The Mind is so near itself – it cannot see, distinctly – and I have none to ask –*

*Should you think it breathed – and had you the leisure to tell me, I should feel quick gratitude –*

*If I make the mistake – that you dared to tell me – would give me sincerer honor – toward you –*

*I enclose my name – asking you, if you please – Sir – to tell me what is true?*

*That you will not betray me – it is needless to ask – since Honor is it's own pawn –*

The brilliantly original opening gambit, asking him if he has time to let her know if her work is 'alive' (echoing language associated with childbirth), struck a chord with Higginson, who recognised in her at all times a profound originality, albeit he found her excessively eccentric. Typically, Emily places her admired correspondent in a position of almost deific responsibility, asking him to let her know what is 'true', as if she herself is a hopeless child, who cannot herself know. On a more pedestrian level, like many writers, she feels too close to the work to judge its worth. Her mind was too 'near itself'. In place of a signature, Emily enclosed a card in its own envelope on which she wrote her name. Also of note is the employment of the same phrase as that used in her letter to Samuel Bowles, of around the same time: 'Honor is it's own pawn –'.

Higginson must have replied swiftly, with literary comment ('surgery' as she experienced it), as well as a number of questions about the author's circumstances and her reading matter. She had caught his interest. Emily replied fully on 25th April 1862. Again, this is an important letter.

*Mr Higginson,*

*Your kindness claimed earlier gratitude – but I was ill – and write today, from my pillow.*

*Thank you for the surgery – it was not so painful as I supposed. I bring you others – as you ask – though they might not differ –*

*While my thought is undressed – I can make the distinction, but when I put them in the Gown – they look alike, and numb.*

*You asked how old I was? I made no verse – but one or two – until this winter – Sir –*

*I had a terror – since September – I could tell to none – and so I sing, as the Boy does by the Burying Ground – because I am afraid – You inquire my Books – For Poets – I have Keats – and Mr and Mrs Browning. For Prose – Mr Ruskin – Sir Thomas Browne – and the Revelations. I went to school – but in your manner of the phrase – had no education. When a little Girl, I had a friend, who taught me Immortality – but venturing too near, himself – he never returned – Soon after, my Tutor, died – and for several years, my Lexicon – was my only companion – Then I found one more – but he was not contented I be his scholar – so he left the Land.*

*You ask of my Companions Hills – Sir – and the Sundown – and a Dog – large as myself, that my Father bought me – They are better than Beings – because they know – but do not tell – and the noise in the Pool, at Noon – excels my Piano. I have a Brother and Sister – My Mother does not care for thought – and Father, too busy with his Briefs – to notice what we do – He buys me many Books – but begs me not to read them – because he fears they joggle the Mind. They are religious – except me – and address an Eclipse, every morning – whom they call their "Father." But I fear my story fatigues you – I would like to learn – Could you tell me how to grow – or is it unconveyed – like Melody – or Witchcraft?*

*You speak of Mr Whitman – I never read his Book – but was told that he was disgraceful –*

*I read Miss Prescott's "Circumstance,"* [A short story by Harriet Prescott Spofford published in *The Atlantic Monthly*, May 1860.] *but it followed me, in the Dark – so I avoided her –*

*Two Editors of Journals came to my Father's House, this winter – and asked me for my Mind – and when I asked them "Why," they said I was penurious – and they, would use it for the World –*

*I could not weigh myself – Myself –*

*My size felt small – to me – I read your Chapters in the Atlantic – and experienced honor for you – I was sure you would not reject a confiding question –*

*Is this – Sir – what you asked me to tell you?*

*Your friend,*

*E – Dickinson.*

The further enclosed poems were 'There came a Day – at Summer's full –', 'Of all the Sounds despatched abroad' and 'South winds jostle them –'. It is noteworthy that Emily sent him some of her weakest and least disturbing work such as 'South winds jostle them –', which reads:

*South winds jostle them –*
*Bumblebees come –*
*Hover – hesitate –*
*Drink, and are gone –*

*Butterflies pause*
*On their passage Cashmere –*
*I – softly plucking,*
*Present them here!*

It is impossible to know what Higginson might have felt had she sent immediately the potent 'He put the Belt around my life –/

I heard the Buckle snap –', or 'The Soul has Bandaged moments –/When too appalled to stir –', and interesting that Emily, who did not hold back with many correspondents, 'spared' him her more extreme expressions at first. Higginson has been criticised by posterity for failing to champion Emily's work sufficiently while she was alive, helping with the publication of her work after her death, but Emily perhaps, by feeling that the darker, often more powerful work may have caused alarm, perhaps did not play her strongest cards as she entered this relationship.

There are many things one could pick up from the compressed and powerful lines of this second letter: her reference to the literary 'surgery' not being as painful as she had feared and her series of false statements; the emotionally defended claim that she had written but 'one or two' poems from before the winter of 1861–2, whereas in fact we know that more than 300 existed; the assertion that her only reading matter was Keats, Browne, Browning, Ruskin and the Revelations (an incomplete picture to say the least); and her statement, emotionally true at times perhaps but inaccurate, that her only companions are 'Sundown – and a Dog –'.

It is understandable that she found it nerve-racking to expose her work in so direct a manner to an eminent writer and critic, and that for Higginson she adopted a highly self-conscious, manufactured literary persona. In this same, densely rich missive are the often-quoted reference to her father as being 'too busy with his Briefs' to notice what she does and the sweeping statement concerning her mother, that she 'does not care for thought'. These pithy summings up are beautifully crafted, and no doubt contain some truth of feeling if not of fact, but they also teach us that we need to safeguard against any single interpretation of anything that Emily says. Martha Dickinson Bianchi issues an interesting warning in her memoir, that '*nothing* could be more fatal to knowing aunt Emily on her own terms than to take her literally when her mood was hyperbolic,' and as Higginson later writes to the poet, she likes to 'shroud' herself in a 'fiery mist'.

Emily's reference to a 'terror – since September' has been the subject of much speculation by commentators. Also of note is the fact that she asks Higginson how to 'grow', as if at the age of thirty-one maturational and educational processes are still eluding her. In relation to the 'terror' that causes her to 'sing' aloud, there have been many theories. These range from those we have considered relating to her psychological state, to the notion that fear for her eyesight caused her to be afraid. We shall consider her eyesight in the next chapter.

In fact, we shall never know to what exactly she referred when she mentioned 'September' in such dramatic terms, nor, judging by the poetic freedom she takes with the truth in the rest of the letter, whether it could be dated to September, or indeed whether the 'terror' was a terror, or less than that, or more than that. Frustratingly perhaps, so much can never be known.

On 7th June another letter was sent to Higginson, revealing that she had received some more criticism from him. This 'surprised' and may have hurt her, yet she also expresses profound gratitude for his attention. Having told him that 'I have had few pleasures so deep as your opinion, and if I tried to thank you, my tears would block my tongue –', and told him about her friend Ben Newton, the 'dying Tutor' who believed she could be a poet, she goes on to say:

*Your second letter surprised me, and for a moment, swung – I had not supposed it. Your first – gave no dishonor, because the True – are not ashamed – I thanked you for your justice – but could not drop the Bells whose jingling cooled my Tramp – Perhaps the Balm, seemed better, because you bled me, first.*

*I smile when you suggest that I delay "to publish" – that being foreign to my thought, as Firmament to Fin –*

*If fame belonged to me, I could not escape her – if she did not, the longest day would pass me on the chase – and the approbation of my Dog, would forsake me – then – My Barefoot-Rank is better –*

*You think my gait "spasmodic" – I am in danger – Sir –*
*You think me "uncontrolled" – I have no Tribunal.*

*Would you have time to be the "friend" you should think I need? I have a little shape – it would not crowd your Desk – nor make much Racket as the Mouse, that dents your Galleries...*

*But, will you be my Preceptor, Mr Higginson?*
*Your friend*
*E – Dickinson*

Higginson has clearly told her that she lacks discipline (is 'uncontrolled') and has a 'spasmodic' gait, an erratic and unpredictable sense of scansion and rhythm, and presumably what he considered an inadequate sense for rhyme. Of course, it is now considered that her avoidance of obvious rhyme, and her preference for employing haunting, accentuating half- or even quarter-rhymes at key moments, is another hallmark of her original genius. An example of such a half rhyme, employed to great effect, is that we have recently witnessed in the poem 'I felt a Funeral, in my Brain,' when she rhymes the lines in the last verse: 'And I dropped down, and down –' with 'And Finished knowing – then –'. The abrupt, blank finality of the suspended 'then', an apparently weak word, which makes for a surprising and potent ending, partly because of the way in which it cuts sharply across our ears semi-rhymed with the word 'down', is precisely the kind of effect that would have disturbed many contemporary readers, and which grip so many of us today.

Emily, perhaps put on the defensive by his comments, states in response to Higginson's suggestion that she delay publication until she has better mastered her poetic gift (advice for which he has often been held at fault), that publication is as 'foreign to my thought, as Firmament to Fin –' – deftly displaying in this surreal, alliterative heterogeneity alone why she deserved publication. Her 'Barefoot – Rank', she says, 'is better'. This is a stance echoed in the often-cited poem about fame, in which she declares it to be undesirable:

> *I'm Nobody! Who are you?*
> *Are you – Nobody – too?*
> *Then there's a pair of us!*
> *Don't tell! they'd advertise – you know!*
>
> *How dreary – to be – Somebody!*
> *How public – like a Frog –*
> *To tell one's name – the livelong June –*
> *To an admiring Bog!*

If Emily had hoped that Higginson would support her in a more professional approach to getting published, it seems as if his response had reconfirmed her in part defensive, and in part genuinely superior, view that for the time being at least, it was best to continue without public approbation. Humbly, however, she also continues to seek his advice. He must have suggested she needed a teacher, for Emily asks him directly if he will be her 'Preceptor'. Hereafter she will often refer to him as her tutor. Although he did not take on any systematic approach to teaching her, Higginson remained a critical friend, in both senses of the word, and went to visit her, twice.

Higginson was curious to meet Emily. A visit to Amherst was set back when in early 1863 he went to South Carolina to be in command of a Negro regiment, to help the cause of slaves whose fight for freedom was a key element of the Civil War. In June 1869, Higginson wrote her a moving letter, one that gives us a touching insight into how she was viewed by her contemporary. As it is one of the few in-depth reactions we have to Emily's writing and persona, it is worth examining. It gives us a sense of the mysterious power Emily emanated, her gift at captivating the mind of another, albeit in a bemusing way, through writing alone.

*Sometimes I take out your letters & verses, dear friend, and when I feel their strange power, it is not strange that I find it hard to write & that long months pass. I have the greatest desire to see you, always feeling that perhaps if I could once take you by the hand I might be something to you; but till then you only enshroud yourself in this fiery mist & I cannot reach you, but only rejoice in the rare sparkles of light. Every year I think that I will contrive somehow to go to Amherst & see you: but that is hard, for I often am obliged to go away... I should like to hear from you very often, but feel always timid lest what I* write *should be badly aimed & miss that fine edge of thought which you bear. It would be so easy, I fear, to miss you. Still, you see, I try...*

*It is hard [for me] to understand how you can live s[o alo]ne, with thoughts of such a [quali]ty coming up in you & even the companionship of your dog withdrawn. Yet it isolates one anywhere to think beyond a certain point or have such luminous flashes as come to you – so perhaps the place does not make much difference.*

Carlo, Emily's dog, to which reference is made, had died in early January 1866 or late 1865. Higginson had received a terse, bereft note in late January saying simply 'Carlo died – /E. Dickinson/Would you instruct me now?' Unsettled by Emily's tendency to solitude (even more pronounced in her epistolary versions of herself than in reality), he urges her to do as 'All ladies do' and visit Boston, where she might see him. Her reply includes a famous sentence, which refers to her never leaving her 'Father's ground'. She also comments that Higginson had been unaware that when he replied to her first letter he had 'saved' her life, and picks up on his commenting about her solitude:

*You noticed my dwelling alone – To an Emigrant, Country is idle except it be his own. You speak kindly of seeing me. Could it please your convenience to come so far as Amherst I should be very glad, but I do not cross my Father's ground to any House or town.*

*Of our greatest acts we are ignorant –*

*You were not aware that you saved my Life. To thank you in person has been since then one of my few requests.*

Higginson did not get around to visiting his 'half-cracked poetess', as his wife unkindly described her, until Tuesday 16th August 1870, eight years after her first letter to him. The night before he sent a note saying he would come to see her, Emily dreamed, she told Higginson, bizarrely, all night of his wife, of whose existence she became aware through a reference made to her in a literary review. Emily had been involved in emotional triangles all her life, often befriending both husband and wife in a couple, as she did with Mr and Mrs Bowles and Mr and Mrs Holland.

In July 1862 she had written to her new friend, 'I had no portrait, now, but am small, like the Wren, and my Hair is bold, like the Chestnut Bur – and my eyes, like the Sherry in the Glass, that the Guest leaves – Would this do just as well?'

After this visit to her, Higginson writes up a long description of their meeting, for his wife. It may have been that he felt he needed to share his experience in order to mitigate any envy his wife might have had over his interest in this intriguing writer, but what he says provides a detailed and disturbing portrait of the poet at this time. It also tells us much about the strange power that the growing 'Myth' (as she was later described by some) was able to exude. She often refers to spells, and it seems clear that she was able to cast her own.

*I shan't sit up tonight to write all about E.D. dearest but if you had read Mrs. Stoddard's novels you could understand a house where each member runs his or her own selves.* [Mrs Stoddard was a popular Gothic novelist.] *Yet I only saw her.*

*A large county lawyer's house, brown brick, with great trees & a garden – I sent up my card. A parlor dark & cool & stiffish, a few books & engravings & an open piano – Malbone & O D* [Out Door] *Papers among other books.*

*A step like a pattering child's in entry & in glided a little plain woman with two smooth bands of reddish hair & a face a little like Belle Dove's; not plainer – with no good feature – in a very plain and exquisitely clean white pique & a blue net worsted shawl. She came to me with two day lilies which she put in a sort of childlike way into my hand & said "These are my introduction" in a soft frightened breathless childlike voice – & added under her breath Forgive me if I am frightened; I never see strangers & hardly know what I say – but she talked soon & thenceforward continuously – & deferentially – sometimes stopping to ask me to talk instead of her – but readily recommencing.*

Among the things she said, all fascinating, he recorded, 'When I lost the use of my Eyes it was a comfort to think there were so few real *books* that I could easily find some one to read me all of them,' and, 'I find ecstasy in living – the mere sense of living is joy enough'. Most interestingly of all, perhaps, he writes:

*I asked if she never felt want of employment, never going off the place & never seeing any visitor "I never thought of conceiving that I could ever have the slightest approach to such a want in all future time" (& added) "I feel that I have not expressed myself strongly enough."*

This statement is rightly famous, and a strong signifier for those who wish to see Emily Dickinson as a woman in control of her own destiny, as opposed to an unfortunately neurotic artist, that she was in control of the way she lived her life.

Twenty years later, in October 1891, Higginson wrote in *The Atlantic Monthly LXVIII* of Emily that:

The impression undoubtedly made on me was that of an excess of tension, and of an abnormal life... Certainly I should have been most glad to bring it down to the level

> of simple truth and every-day comradeship; but it was not altogether easy. She was much too enigmatical a being for me to solve in an hour's interview, and an instinct told me that the slightest attempt at direct cross-examination would make her withdraw into her shell…

Higginson visited again, in early December 1873, declaring to his sisters in a letter that:

> *I saw my eccentric poetess Miss Emily Dickinson who* never *goes outside her father's grounds & sees only me & a few others. She says, "there is always one thing to be grateful for – that one is one's self & not somebody else" but* [my wife] *Mary thinks this is singularly out of place in E.D.'s case… I'm afraid Mary's other remark "Oh why do the insane so cling to you?' still holds.*

Is my verse "alive"? was Emily's first question to Higginson. Whilst he tried to refine the rawness of her art, asking her to iron out the livid presence of her dashes, the bewildering under-cutting of anticipated traditional rhythm and rhyme that in fact make it so 'alive', he was nonetheless a lifeline for the poet, a loyal correspondent until her death in 1886. Beyond death he continued to be a friend, aiding, if occasionally uncertainly, her publication and posthumous reputation.

# 'I have done with guises'
# Late years at home

In 1864 to 1865 Emily had had to spend many months in Cambridge, Boston, to be treated by Boston's most eminent ophthalmologist Dr Henry Willard Williams. During that time she stayed with her treasured cousins, Louisa and Frances Norcross. The nature of the complaint is not recorded. Some think it to have been exotropia ('wall-eyed vision'); Habegger argues a case for anterior uveitis (rheumatic iritis) which causes great pain and intolerance of light and yet can be treated and clear up almost completely; Cody and Garbowsky both argue for the causes being largely psychosomatic; and Gordon more recently that it was linked to epilepsy. Whatever the nature of the ailment, it caused Emily unhappiness, and upset on behalf of those who loved her at home. Emily was not allowed to read for a prolonged period. She told Higginson that the first writer whose work she read after her eye treatment was Shakespeare. Her cousins had probably entertained her with lively renditions of his work, as they were keen amateur actors who often read his work out loud. We know that Emily became an ardent fan of *Anthony and Cleopatra*, and *Henry VI part 1*, and *Othello* soon after. We also know that Emily's father admired Shakespeare, although at the same time he was able to imagine his family's superseding the English genius, for Emily had written many years earlier to Austin, on 6th July 1851, aged twenty, 'Father says your letters are altogether before Shakespeare, and he will have them published to put in our library.' The irony that it was his daughter, and not his son, who reached the literary heights, is not to be lost.

When Emily returned to Amherst in 1865 she did not, as far as we know, leave home before her death in 1886. She seems to have settled into a quiet, domestic routine that continued to include making the bread for which she was known within the family, and the highly skilled tending of the garden and herbarium. A handyman Tim became her ally and helped get notes to Susan over at the Evergreens. After years of internal tension and her eye troubles, it appears that the poet needed to convalesce.

From the middle to the end of the 1860s Emily Dickinson's poetic Muse lay dormant, although it was never inactive, and she stopped her practice of collating her work in notebooks in 1865, not resuming for six years. She produced relatively little poetry, kept on loose sheets and scraps of paper, and fewer letters. The verse she does write seems quieter. The rampaging terror of mental anguish, and ecstasy of heightened passion, recede and she seems to view tumult through a more distant lens. Noteworthy during her correspondence in this period are the letters to Higginson, some of which we have seen, and notes written to Susan, often still passionate, although more concise, and with a sense of distance. Tender correspondence was also maintained with Louisa and Frances Norcross, the cousins in Boston she dearly loved.

Emily's only niece, Martha, was born in 1866. Although Martha and Emily's relationship seems less tender than the poet's became with her nephews – especially with the youngest, born after her niece – nonetheless Martha was to play a major role in helping to forge her aunt's posthumous reputation.

Martha, as we have established, wrote a memoir, *Emily Dickinson: Face to Face*, which was published in 1932, partly with the 'agenda' of reinstating her mother Susan in a picture from which she had been bowdlerised by Austin and his lover (who between them had literally cut Susan's name out of various letters and kept poetry about her at bay). Nonetheless Emily's niece provides insights into the withdrawn years that Emily spent at home. One of Martha's main points is that contrary to rumour, Emily engaged with Susan on loving terms until the last. Indeed, this view is borne out by the missives Emily continued to send to Susan, some of which we have seen. Martha also describes how the two held private meetings in the North-west Passage, a secret passage that lay between the kitchen and the middle hall in the Homestead, and grabbed time to discuss Emily's work and exchange intimacies when they could.

Sue and Austin's daughter also recalls the extreme power that her grandfather held, and the double life that his daughters led: irreverent and high-spirited behind his back, falling into a sober mode at the insistence of their mother when he returned. She is also a source of insight into Emily's withdrawal, and the fascination it created in others, commenting that local people would 'boast' of glimpsing Emily, and that whilst Emily could live happily enough without them, they found it impossible to stop wanting to engage with her.

Far from becoming invisible, Emily, whether unconsciously or not, had by her withdrawal made herself a centre of attention in a most dramatic way. Martha says of her father Austin that, 'He could never reconcile himself to her way of living that brought such ridiculous conjecture upon her. He would have wished her happy and natural – although even in the same breath he could never wish her any different!' It is clear that her brother worried about her, although he continued to trust her as a confidante.

Three people that did see Emily recorded their visit in February 1877. The singer Nora Green and two of her siblings came to the Homestead to give a private singing performance. Vinnie had seen them perform and liked them, and Emily must have invited them to their home. When they arrived, they record, no one was in sight, but the Greens guessed they were to go ahead and sing, which they did. Afterwards, 'a light clapping of hands… floated down the staircase, and Miss Lavinia came to tell us that Emily would see us – my sister and myself – in the library.' She, as Higginson had done, noted a childlike figure, 'a tiny figure in white' who 'darted to greet us, grasped our hands, and told us of her pleasure in hearing us', she spoke breathlessly, and told them she used to play the piano herself.

It is a confusing picture of Emily that emerges in this mid-late period, of a woman apparently in control, regally demanding the presence of chosen visitors, yet at the same time unable to engage with them face to face in a sustained way, and socially vulnerable.

A final observation of Martha's, too intriguing not to refer to, that her aunt moved often in a state of 'revery', 'flitting always', muttering to herself like 'an unconscious artist'. Although this description of Emily 'flitting' has been criticised as sentimental, possibly inaccurate and helping to stoke the image of the poet as ethereal and unreal in ways modern critics find belittling, it is nonetheless convincing that we see Emily brimful with words. Word-play and inspirations, in her niece's retrospective view, seem here to bubble out of her, and it is likely that her mind was often still preoccupied with the articulation of her inner life.

Between the years of 1871 and 1875 Emily resumed her practice of collating her poetry into notebooks, an activity she had stopped in 1865. Some have called the poetry collected in these fascicles a period of late flowering. Beyond 1875 she never collected work in the same way, but she did still go on writing, producing in the region of a further 400 poems between then and her death eleven years later.

The first cataclysm to interrupt Emily's routine was the death of her father on 15th June 1874. Edward, already aged seventy-one, was in Boston working when he grew faint. He then suffered an 'apoplectic attack' – a stroke – was prescribed opium or morphine, and died later that day. This gargantuan loss devastated the household, marked the end of an era and in some ways, as we shall see, made room for the Dickinson children to behave in ways that some felt lacked decorum.

Death was followed by birth, and on 1st August 1875, a second nephew, Thomas Gilbert, known as Gib, was born: Susan and Austin's last child and Austin's favourite. Emily, far less jealous of the children than she had been when Ned first arrived, enjoyed their stories and lively influence within the grounds of the Homestead. Gib in particular was thought to have the Dickinson stamp of quirky, irresistible brilliance.

Yet this much adored child was to die early, at just eight years old on October 5th 1883. This loss, which took Emily over the few hundred yards to the Evergreens for the first time 'in fifteen years' according to records by Vinnie, was to prove a final sorrow that weakened Emily's reserves. Moreover, other troubles were brewing. Life at the Evergreens had not been happy, and it was about to get more tortured still. Just after Gib's death, Austin, aged fifty-three consolidated a passionate love affair with Mabel Todd, a married woman over twenty years his junior.

A few years on from Gib's birth in 1878 Emily's great friend, the irrepressible editor and lover of gifted women Samuel Bowles, died, greatly weakened after a series of catastrophic events in his own life. Shortly before this, in June of the same year according to a story later told by Vinnie, he had visited Emily. At first, Vinnie remembered, her sister refused to see him. Bowles however yelled up at her, 'Emily, you wretch! No more of this nonsense!... Come down at once.' To Vinnie's surprise, Emily did come down and was 'fascinating'.

A few years later she did not agree to see an old friend, Emily Fowler Ford, when she came by in 1882. A poem by Emily Fowler Ford, written five years after the poet's death in 1891, and published in *The Sunday Republican*, Brooklyn, 3rd January, 1891, gives an intriguing glimpse into one view of Emily Dickinson at that time. Lines include:

*Nor will you touch a hand, or greet a face, –*
*For common daily strife to you is rude,*
*And, shrinking, you in shadow lonely stay*
*Invisible to all, howe'er we pray.*

Yet for Emily, alongside an increasing number of debilitating, late losses, was a degree of late joy. Two new relationships in particular were a source of pleasure, engagement and intensity. Emily came to know Helen Fiske Hunt Jackson, the daughter of Nathan Welby Fiske, a professor of moral philosophy and metaphysics at Amherst College. Helen Hunt was herself a leading American writer. She had married twice: Edward Bissell Hunt, and, after his death in 1863, William S. Jackson in 1875. Emily had come across her as a child when Helen had lived in Amherst, but the poets were reunited through Higginson.

Higginson sent Emily some of Helen's poetry and Emily replied strongly, that 'Mrs Hunt's Poems are stronger than any written by Women since Mrs – Browning, with the exception of Mrs Lewes –'. Helen and Emily began to correspond in 1875, and the former, with bold clarity, being one of the only people to see clearly the poet's stature within her lifetime, wrote to Emily, 'I have a little manuscript volume with a few of your verses in it – and I read them very often – You are a great poet – and it is a wrong to the day you live in, that you will not sing aloud. When you are what men call dead, you will be sorry you were so stingy.'

Helen, convinced of Emily's talents, wrote again and asked Emily if she would allow her to send some of the verses she possessed (no doubt through her connection with Higginson) to a circular to which she was contributing, with a view to anonymous publication. Jackson visited Emily two months later, a visit Martha recalls with vivid excitement in her memoir, and urged her again to allow her to publish. Emily writes in alarm to Higginson, saying that she had had a visit from Jackson, who did not seem to take it seriously when she had said she was 'unwilling' to publish because 'I was incapable'. Apparently during her visit, Helen had robustly commented that she looked unwell and reprimanded her. Later she wrote apologising, in a fascinating letter that gives us another perspective on Emily's oddly insubstantial physical presence.

> *[I feel] as if I ha[d been] very imperti[nent that] day [in] speaking to you [as] I did, – accusing you of living away from the sunlight – and [telling] you that you [looke]d ill... but re[al]ly you look[ed] so [wh]ite and [mo]th-like [!] Your [hand] felt [l]ike such a wisp in mine that you frigh[tened] me.*

Emily, despite feeling incapable, must have capitulated to her friend's demand, for on 8th December 1878 Helen wrote thanking Emily for allowing 'Success is counted sweetest' to be published in the journal *A Masque of Poets*. According to Martha, who wrote about this incident in *Face to Face*, when Susan showed Emily the printed poem the poet turned so white she wished she had not let her see it.

Helen Hunt asked to be Dickinson's literary executor and one can only imagine how much less troubled the posthumous path to publication may have been had this come about. Instead, the irrepressible, far-sighted Hunt Jackson was to die tragically young, from stomach cancer, it is thought, following a complication with a leg injury caused by a fall, in 1885. Emily wrote to Higginson that she was 'unspeakably shocked' to learn she was on the point of death, and in late August wrote a condolence letter to Mr Jackson. 'Helen of Troy will die, but Helen of Colorado, never... I never saw Mrs Jackson but twice, but those twice are indelible...'

In 1880, Emily was given a marbled Shakespeare concordance by the man who became her last and possibly only 'real', reciprocal love; and in the same year, she was visited for the second and last time by Charles Wadsworth – the man whom many think to have been the 'Master'. With Helen Hunt's clear vision of Emily's greatness, and a flesh-and-blood companion, it seems that a few seeds were sown that were to bear late fruit, while some remaining questions were seeking resolution.

Emily's lover was in some ways an unlikely candidate and in others, the epitome of all she most respected in a man. Otis Phillips Lord, an elderly judge on the Massachusetts Supreme Judicial Court and eighteen years Emily's senior, was described by Emily as her father's 'best' friend. He and his wife had come to stay for a week in 1875, the year following Edward's death in 1874. This visit must have been of critical importance to Emily, bereft as she was. The Lords were family friends of some importance and long standing, and he would have been a reassuring presence at the Homestead. It is not known exactly when he and Emily first acknowledged more than friendly affection for one another, and theories abound as to when exactly their love affair began, some dating it to as early as 1872 or 1873, but it seems most likely that any romantic feelings they held for one another would have been held in abeyance until the moment came when it was respectable (as near as this was possible) to declare otherwise.

In 1877, Lord's wife died. In 1880 he made his first visit to Amherst without her. This seems the likely time for his late love affair with Emily Dickinson to have begun.

The first letter we have of hers to him (originally dated by Johnson as being 'about 1878') is astonishing and beautiful. It is full of open expression and a palpable sense of emotional relief.

*My lovely Salem smiles at me. I seek his Face so often – but I have done with guises.*

*I confess that I love him – I rejoice that I love him – I thank the maker of Heaven and Earth – that gave him me to love – the exultation floods me.*

The arrangement the couple seemed to come to was, when apart, to write every Sunday. Emily's mother died on 14th November 1882, and soon after it appears that Lord asked Emily to marry him, for she writes to him in a letter of 3rd December of the same year:

> *The Month in which our Mother died, closed it's Drama Thursday, and I cannot conjecture a form of space without her timid face.*
>
> *... You said with loved timidity in asking me to your dear Home, you would "try not to make it unpleasant." So delicate a diffidence, how beautiful to see!*

Emily would refuse any offer, in whatever spirit it had been made (earnestly and/or out of loving anxiety). It must have been gratifying to have experienced such devotion, and their affair was clearly potent enough to be a source of deep anxiety to Lord's niece who complained – adding to the picture of Emily as a complex, multi-faceted and unique individual – that Emily was a 'Little hussy' and 'crazy about men'. Their intimacy continued in letters and occasional meetings until Lord's death in 1884. Passion for a 'Master' seems to have been resolved with a real, mutual relationship with a powerful older man.

When Emily ordered Vinnie to burn her letters, she specifically retained drafts of letters written to Otis Lord. When she was buried, Higginson records in his diary that he saw at the funeral Vinnie put two heliotropes in the coffin by hand, for Emily 'to take to Judge Lord'.

Resolution with Wadsworth it seems was also due. We know that by autumn 1876 she was once more in touch with him, and that in the summer of 1880 he came to Amherst to see her for a second and last time. We have a record from Vinnie who says she was tending her flowers when she heard him speaking to the servant, Maggie. She said to her sister, 'the Gentleman with the deep voice wants to see you, Emily.' Emily showed 'glad surprise'. We know little more about their exchange, other than that he informed his friend that he had a serious throat illness and was liable to die at any time. Wadsworth did die, two years later, on 1st April 1882. She writes to Lord, 'my Philadelphia has passed from Earth'. Martha Dickinson Bianchi recorded in her memoir that Emily had told Susan about her love of Wadsworth, and that Susan had kept it a secret. This is discredited as a source, but nonetheless intriguing.

Emily's ongoing relationship during these late years with Susan is also, as has been stated, important. In 1874 Emily wrote a devastating poem about her sister-in-law, which she apparently later tried to destroy. The first four lines run:

> *Now I knew I lost her –*
> *Not that she was gone –*
> *But Remoteness travelled*
> *On her Face and Tongue.*

This is one of the most enduringly powerful of Emily's poems about Sue, revealing the degree of difficulty the poet had when faith in Sue – or indeed any idealised person – was in jeopardy. Musing on her faltering connection she concludes:

> *His is Penury*
> *Not who toils for Freedom*
> *Or for Family*
> *But the Restitution*
> *Of Idolatry.*

We recall that Emily had written to Susan almost twenty years earlier, 'Few have been given me, and if I love them so, that for *idolatory*, they are removed from me – I simply murmur *gone*'.

It seems that Emily's struggle with her powerful, idealised feelings for Susan was never resolved. She could never quite let her go, for Emily continued to express to her that she held a position of ultimate power. Many notes were sent to Susan, after this poem about disillusion, that reinstate her as the most important person in Emily's life. The most potent of these is a simple line, sent in the same year as the poem.

> *"Egypt – thou knew'st" –*

This is a quote from Shakespeare's *Anthony and Cleopatra*, the play Emily cited most often and which she revered. Susan would also have known it. The full meaning of Emily's single line is revealed through an extended quotation:

> *Egypt, though knew'st too well,*
> *My heart was to thy rudder tied by the strings,*
> *And thou shouldst tow me after. O'er my spirit*
> *Thy full supremacy thou knew'st, and that*
> *Thy beck might from the bidding of the gods*
> *Command me.*

Susan's relationship with Austin, however, had deteriorated to an alarming degree. To add to the misery of the couple, as has been mentioned, their youngest child Gib died in October 1883. It is thought that grief over this tragic loss hastened his aunt Emily's demise some two and half years later, and further contributed to Austin's desire for solace. In 1882, Austin had begun his love affair with Mabel Loomis Todd, the much younger wife of promiscuous David Todd, who was a graduate of Amherst College and who returned there as astronomy teacher in 1881. The affair between his wife and Emily's brother was consummated, according to Gordon, after Gib's death, in 1883. It became an intensely passionate, openly conducted liaison, destructive to the Dickinson family life, and lasting thirteen years, until Austin's death.

When David Todd had moved back to Amherst, newcomer Mabel, enchanting, clever and unorthodox, had begun as a favourite of Sue's – and indeed a platonic lover of her son Ned's. The complexity of what followed was scandalous and fascinating, and, inevitably, affected Emily, who, along with Vinnie, became her brother's confidante on a daily basis. This was an extraordinary relationship, with profound implications for Emily. The main impact was perhaps posthumous, in that the love affair helped increase tensions between the Homestead and the Evergreens, to the extent that Susan and Vinnie were in time to become bitter enemies. After Emily's death there were to be years of scrabbling for supremacy between Susan and her daughter, and Mabel Loomis Todd and her daughter Millicent Todd Bingham, in relation to the poet's legacy. For an in-depth study of these family relations see Sewall's chapter 'War Between the Houses' in his biography *The Life of Emily Dickinson* and Gordon's *Lives Like Loaded Guns: Emily Dickinson and her Family's Feuds*.

The story of Emily's last few years continued with the death, in March 1884, of Otis Lord himself, which left Emily ever more bereft. She writes soon after the loss to Charles H. Clark referring to Lord as 'another cherished friend', adding 'how to repair my shattered ranks is a besetting pain'; and to cousins Louisa and Frances Norcross, the suffering poet writes, 'I hardly dare to know that I have lost another friend, but anguish finds it out.'

A late poem offers crucial comment about this last period of her life.

*My Wars are laid away in Books –*
*I have one Battle more –*
*A Foe whom I have never seen*
*But oft has scanned me o'er -*
*And hesitated me between*

*And others at my side,*
*But chose the best – Neglecting me – till*
*All the rest have died –*
*How sweet if I am not forgot*
*By Chums that passed away –*
*Since Playmates at threescore and ten*
*Are such a scarcity*

On 15th May 1886, Emily herself gave way. The cause given was Bright's disease, a term no longer in use that referred to kidney disease; most modern biographers agree that the true cause seems likely to have been severe primary hypertension, caused by excessive strain. Susan took charge of the funeral, at which was read 'No Coward Soul is Mine' by Emily Brontë. There is no record of 'Egypt's' presence at the occasion she planned: Susan was avoiding Austin and his lover Mabel Todd, who did attend.

## *How sweet if I am not forgot*
## Posthumous Legacy

*Titled – Confirmed –*
*Delirious Charter!*
*Mine – long as Ages steal!*

For almost the entirety of her recorded life, Emily had displayed a 'special' relationship with the afterlife. She had, as we have seen, explored in her letters and poetry, over and over again, questions of 'what happens next?' What happened next in the immediate aftermath of her death was that Vinnie discovered the chest of poetry and as instructed, burned the letters that were sent to Emily, including her drafts to others, with the exception of those to Otis Lord that Emily had retained.

Vinnie's first choice of editor was Susan, and she gave the manuscripts to her sister-in-law to select and edit. Within a two-year period, however, Susan had apparently achieved little on behalf of her sister's reputation, despite forays made to publishers by Susan in which she sent individual poems. It is important to remember that Susan, who had so often championed and critiqued Emily's work during her lifetime, would have been grieving the loss, as well as being troubled by her own life's circumstances. Her husband's love affair with Mabel had become a public scandal. In addition, Susan may have been dubious as to the wisdom of trawling around sceptical publishers with the work of a recluse, whose writing the family had held so precious and which contained so much that was intimate, not least, about herself. Frustrated at the delay, however, Vinnie proceeded to turn to her sister-in-law's arch rival, Austin's lover, Mabel, to edit the work. This move was to spark years of bitter enmity, explored, as has been said, by Sewall and Gordon in particular. Ambitious and brilliant, Mabel had been fascinated by Emily throughout her relationship with Austin. She started work on the poems as a copyist, yet as she worked, she became increasingly absorbed by Emily's poetic legacy. Together, she and Vinnie persuaded Higginson to help them, and by November 1890 the first selection of Emily's work, edited by Mabel and Higginson, was ready for publication.

This volume categorised, crudely we now think, the poems into 'Life', 'Love', 'Nature' and 'Time and Eternity', gave the poems titles (which Emily had never given them) and included 'My life closed twice before it's close' and 'He touched me, so I live to know/That such a day, permitted so,/ I groped opon his breast –', one of the many poems associated with 'Master'. In addition, Emily's original grammar was heavily tampered with, in an effort to make the work more acceptable in the editors' views.

A second small volume appeared in 1891 produced by the same editors, including a section from a letter to Emily from Helen Hunt Jackson, of 3rd September 1884, a year before her death, in which she asked to be Emily's Literary Executor, and tells her, 'It is a cruel wrong to your "day & generation" that you will not give them [your poems] light... I do not think we have a right to with hold from the world a word or a thought any more than a *deed,* which might help a single soul.'

A third volume, edited by Mabel, came out in 1896.

Martha Dickinson Bianchi, Susan's daughter, made a rival contribution to Emily's legacy when in 1914 she brought out a volume of the poems Emily had sent to Susan, called *The Single Hound*. Importantly, Martha kept to Emily's own grammar, and according to poet Amy Lowell this was worth 'the other [earlier] three volumes put together'.

Two further volumes edited by Martha Dickinson Bianchi, one including some letters, ensued, culminating with significant success when in 1929 *Further Poems by Emily Dickinson*, edited by Martha and her heir Alfred Leete Hampson, became a best-seller in America. The poet's reputation was made, and would only increase with time. Martha, although partisan to Susan, nonetheless provides introductions that are passionate and articulate. She says, 'Emily's affair with words was her own. She read the dictionary as the rest of her family read the newspaper for the latest news, but no one ever saw her consult it. It was magic to her, not a spelling book.' An exhaustive review of the *Further Poems*, which appeared in the *Revue des Deux Mondes* entitled 'La Vie secrète d'une puritaine' ('The Secret Life of a Puritan'), reveals an increasing excitement about the work, commenting that Emily's 'gems… leave our blunter English dim by comparison'. Critics and readers were beginning to appreciate what Emily had achieved.

As the papers were divided between the Evergreens and Mabel Todd, it was possible for Mabel to produce a volume containing new work, *Bolts of Melody*, in 1945. This was prepared with the help of Mabel's daughter, Millicent Todd Bingham, and its publication ensured that virtually all the works had been published, displaying varying levels of authenticity to the original grammar and wording.

The body of work in the Todd-Bianchi 'camp' was bought by Harvard University from Alfred Leete Hampson in 1955. Millicent Bingham Todd gave her portion of the original manuscripts, however, to a different institution, Amherst College. An agreement made between these two institutions allows the work in Amherst to remain there.

A brilliant three-volume edition of the poems, edited by Thomas H. Johnson, appeared in 1955. This was the first edition of all known poems without alterations. A single-volume edition of this, with its invaluable subject index, came out in 1960. In 1958 he also edited *The Letters of Emily Dickinson.*

More recently, Franklin has reappraised the entire oeuvre, making the first major contribution to Dickinson studies since Johnson. In 1981 he was responsible for *The Manuscript Books of Emily Dickinson* published by The Belknap Press of Harvard University Press. This contains reproductions of the complete original fascicles in Emily's handwriting. As a result of this work Franklin was able to go on to produce a new three-volume edition of the complete poetic oeuvre, *The Poems of Emily Dickinson* (1998) and the single-volume *The Poems of Emily Dickinson: Reading Edition* (1999). These works by Franklin, importantly, follow an updated chronology.

Thanks to all the above editors and volumes of work, alongside others less well known, Dickinson's reputation has now spread worldwide and her greatness been firmly established.

A few invaluable books for those interested in finding out more about Emily Dickinson, most of which have been heavily relied upon as sources for this book, are listed in the bibliography, with many more worth investigating. Most notable among these for people who want to find out more about Emily's life and work are Sewall's two-part biography *The Life of Emily Dickinson*, published in 1974 and Habegger's highly eloquent *My Wars are Laid Away in Books*, 2001.

In addition to these books, Emily Dickinson's life and work have inspired many plays and works of art. Two of the best-known plays are *The Belle of Amherst* by William Luce, which premiered and was published in 1976, and *Emily Dickinson and I: The Journey of a Portrayal* by Jack Lynch and Edie Campbell, premiered in 1999, published in 2005. Her words have been set to music by composers such as Aaron Copeland and Graham Ramsay, and art installations made by artists such as Iza Maciejewska. There is no question but that Emily Dickinson will go on to inspire more artists in all forms, for many generations to come.

## List of works

Poems taken from Ralph W. Franklin
*The Poems of Emily Dickinson: Reading edition*
Cambridge, Mass,: The Belknap Press of Harvard University Press, copyright 1998, 1999

A word made flesh is seldom
I reckon when I count at all
I was the slightest in the house
I like to see it lap the miles
It struck me every
The Lilac is an ancient shrub
The Brain in wider than the sky
The soul selects her own society
In Ebon Box when years have flown
I shall know why when time is over
I heard a fly buzz when I died
Mine by the right of the white election
I think I was enchanted
Awake ye muses nine, sing me a strain divine
It was given to me by the gods
'Tis so much joy! 'Tis so much joy
The Martyr Poets did not tell
Rehearsal to ourselves
One sister have I in the house
Adrift! A little boat adrift
So bashful when I spied her
Is it true, dear Sue?
She dealt her pretty words like blades –
It might be lonelier
I cannot live with you
Me from myself to banish
It struck me every day
Pain has an element of blank

After great pain a formal feeling comes
I felt a cleaving in my mind
The first day's night had come
I felt a funeral in my Brain
South winds jostle them
I'm Nobody! Who are you?
Now I knew I lost her
My wars are laid away in books
Mine by the right of the white election

Poems taken from, *The Letters of Emily Dickinson*
Thomas H. Johnson, Associate Editor Theodora Ward,
Cambridge, Mass,: The Belknap Press of Harvard University,
copyright 1958, 1986

I have a Bird in spring
Safe in their alabaster chambers
Could I then shut the door
Title divine is mine

# Further reading


Martha Dickinson Bianchi, *Emily Dickinson Face to Face: Unpublished Letters with Notes and Reminiscences* (Boston: Houghton Mifflin Company, 1932).

John Cody, *After Great Pain: The Inner Life of Emily Dickinson* (Belknap Press of the Harvard University Press, 1971).

*Emily Dickinson's Herbarium: A Facsimile Edition* (Cambridge, MA and London: The Belknap Press of the Harvard University Press, 2006).

Lillian Faderman, *Surpassing the Love of Men: Romantic Friendship and Love between Women from the Renaissance to Present* (London: Women's Press, 1985).

Lyndall Gordon, *Lives Like Loaded Guns: Emily Dickinson and her Family's Feuds* (London: Virago Press, 2010).

Alfred Habegger, *My Wars Are Laid Away in Books: The Life of Emily Dickinson* (New York: Random House, 2001).

*The Letters of Emily Dickinson*, ed. Thomas Johnson and Theodora V. Ward (Belknap Press of the Harvard University Press, 1958).

*The Manuscript Books of Emily Dickinson*, ed. R.W. Franklin (Belknap Press of the Harvard University Press, 1981).

Cristanne Miller, *Emily Dickinson: A Poet's Grammar* (Harvard University Press, 1987).

*The Poems of Emily Dickinson*, ed. R.W. Franklin (Belknap Press of the Harvard University Press, 1998).

*The Poems of Emily Dickinson, Reading Edition*, ed. R.W. Franklin (Belknap Press of the Harvard University Press, 1999).

*The Poems of Emily Dickinson*, ed. Thomas Johnson (Belknap Press of the Harvard University Press, 1955).

Richard B. Sewall, *The Life of Emily Dickinson* (New York: Farrar, Straus, Giroux, 1974).

# Biographical note

Rebecca Swift read English at Oxford University and has since worked as an editor and writer. For seven years she worked at Virago Press, where she first conceived of the idea for The Literary Consultancy which she co-founded in 1996, and where she is currently Director. For Chatto & Windus she edited a volume of letters between Bernard Shaw and Margaret Wheeler, *Letters from Margaret: The Fascinating Story of Two Babies Swapped at Birth* (1992) and *Imagining Characters: Six Conversations about Women Writers*, a book of conversations between writer A.S. Byatt and psychoanalyst Ignês Sodré (1995). Rebecca has also had poetry published in *Virago New Poets* (1990), *Vintage New Writing 6* (1995), *Driftwood*, US (2005), and *Staple* (2008). A libretto written by Rebecca was funded by the Arts Council England, and commissioned by the Lontano Ensemble: the opera 'Spirit Child', composed by Jenni Roditi, was performed at Ocean in Hackney, London in 2001. Rebecca has also written and reviewed for *The Independent on Sunday* and *The Guardian* and completed an M.A. in Psychoanalytic Studies at the Tavistock.

## Acknowledgements

I would like to thank Daniel Hahn for recommending my passion for Emily Dickinson to Hesperus Press. This passion was first instilled by the late Deborah Kellaway (1922–96), one of those English teachers who enhances lives. Edie Campbell and Jack Lynch, authors of the one woman play 'Emily Dickinson and I; The Journey of a Portrayal' kept the flame burning.

Others to be thanked are Margot Waddell for keeping the faith, Helen Cosis Brown for a patient ear and acute insight, and my mother, Margaret Drabble, who read the first draft, and indicated where my grammatical usage was confusing and unlike Emily's – not so brilliantly. She is also to thank for my interest in literature from when (my) time began. My father Clive Swift and step-father Michael Holroyd, have also deeply influenced my interest in poetry and biography over the years.

Ellie Robins at Hesperus Press has been the kind of editor writers crave: efficient and supportive, and Martha Pooley at Hesperus is also to be thanked.

Critical thanks is also due to previous biographers and critics of Emily Dickinson's work without which of course this compact endeavour would not have been possible. Chief amongst those to whom I feel gratitude are R.B. Sewall, for his remarkable two-volume *The Life of Emily Dickinson*, Alfred Habegger, whose biography *My Wars are Laid Away in Books: The Life of Emily Dickinson* added much to my understanding of her life. All others can be found in the bibliography and acknowledged in the work.

**HESPERUS PRESS**

Hesperus Press is committed to bringing near what is far – far both in space and time. Works written by the greatest authors, and unjustly neglected or simply little known in the English-speaking world, are made accessible through new translations and a completely fresh editorial approach. Through these classic works, the reader is introduced to the greatest writers from all times and all cultures.

For more information on Hesperus Press, please visit our website: **www.hesperuspress.com**